Howard   St Paul Minn. for M. Ives   Dec

R. Bass   Colorado Springs Col. thr Gerrit Smith /   July   2

Mc Cormick   Port Jervis N.Y. ph. to P.E. Farnum Port Jervis   Feb

Schenck   Proprietor of Westminster Hotel   Feb

A Raynor   15 West 36 Str.   Apr   2
from Hamburg to Steinway & Sons London   July
Steinway   C/o Joh. Schroeder Hamburg   Sept   2
Kenefick   9 East 54 St   Joseph O. Fisher   Oct
    New Haven Conn.   5.16 - 5av Dec 15/   Sept

necke   47 East 78 Str.   Sept 9
in 206 W 29 St ph. to Mrs. A. B Jennings Short Hills (this side Summit N.J / June 16
from Providence R.I. dd. to J. H. Richardson
from Hamburg to C. Hartwigh Hamburg
Steinway   C/o Joh. Schroeder Hamburg   Aug 1

Steinert   New Haven Conn.   Oct

Cottier   Buffalo N.Y.   Jan

les   9 East 66 St.   Mch

   San Francisco Cal.   Nov

"Lone Star"
52 Exchge Pl. ph. to W.P. Brownsville by New Orleans R.R.   Jan
Backus (of San Francisco Minstrels) 246 West 44 St. Sept. 28. 1882.
N.Y. first ph. to Glen Cove L.I.   June

Baldwin   426 Bloomfield Str. Hoboken N.J.   Jan
from Hamburg to St Sons, London   May
Steinway C/o Joh. Schroeder Hamburg   Nov
Hilliard   Herbert Barlow E 13 St Oct 10/
McIntoSh   110 Lefferts Place Brooklyn   Jan

WITHDRAWN

Number	Oct	Style	Size	Wood	from	Factory	
3510	7/3	G	4'8"	Eby	Nov	24/80	w.p. hammers.
3511	7/3	G	4'8"	Eby	Dec	4/80	" " "
3512	7/3	G	4'8"	Eby	Dec	31/80	" " "
3513	7/3	G	4'8"	Eby	Jan	14/81	" " "
3514	7/3	G	4'8"	Eby	Jan	7/81	w.p. hammers
3515	7	B	6'8"	Rosd	Sept	25/80	2 pedals. Pillar legs. not fin. Not Var.
3516	7	A	6'	Rosd	Sept	7/81	B rep'd. 8/4/11 ✓
3517	7	A	6'	Rosd	Sept	3/81	At Los Angeles during fire Mar.
3518	7	A	6'	Eby	Feb	28/81	
3519	7	A	6'	Eby	Aug	16/80	Key board. screws, lockboard battis, Key block screws, legs. Pillar legs. complete case with bottom work. strung
3520	7	A	6'	Rosd	Oct	4/81	
3521	7	F	4'4½"	Rosd	Jan	7/81	w.p. hammers,
3522	7	F	4'4½"	Rosd	Mar	2/81	
3523	7	F	4'4½"	Rosd	Jan	5/81	w.p. hammers
3524	7	F	4'4½"	Rosd	Dec	29/81	w.p. hammers,
3525	7	F	4'4½"	Rosd	May	3/81	for.
3526	7	F	4'4½"	Rosd	Jan	8/81	w.p. hammers.
3527	7	A	6'	Rosd	Nov	1/80	2 pedals unfnd

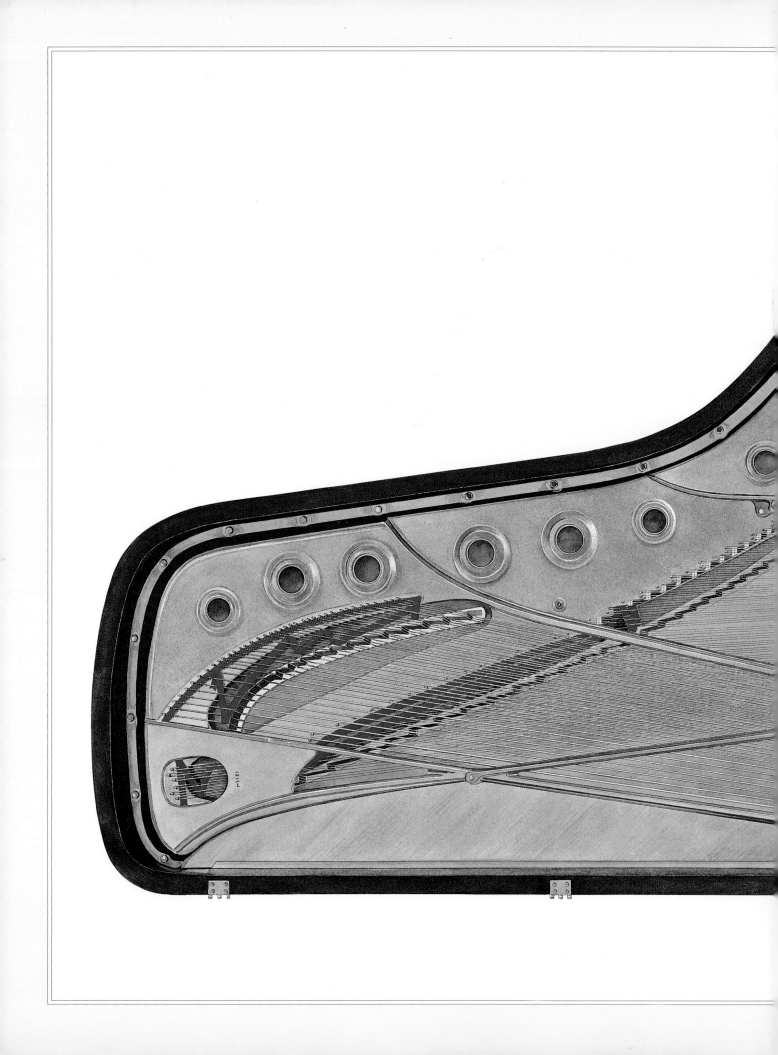

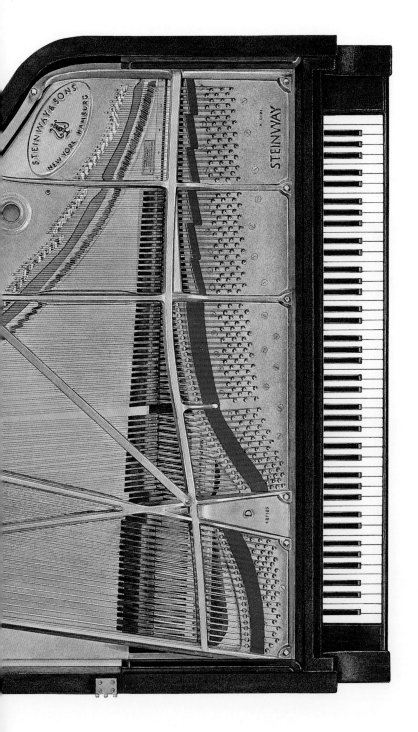

KEYS

*The Making of a
Steinway Piano*

By

MILES CHAPIN

Illustrations by

RODICA PRATO

CLARKSON POTTER/PUBLISHERS
NEW YORK

To the women of the House of Steinway.

Especially Elizabeth Steinway Chapin, numbers one and two.

The author and illustrator gratefully acknowledge the following for granting

permission to use photographs for creating some of the illustrations: Vincent Dente,

Henry Grossman, Richard K. Lieberman, and Leo Spellman.

Musical note excerpts of "I Love a Piano" by Irving Berlin, copyright © 1916 by Irving Berlin.

Copyright renewed. International copyright secured. Used by Permission. All Rights Reserved.

Published by Clarkson N. Potter, Inc., 201 East 50th Street, New York, New York 10022.
Member of the Crown Publishing Group.

Random House, Inc. New York, Toronto, London, Sydney, Auckland

http://www.randomhouse.com/

CLARKSON POTTER, POTTER, and colophon are trademarks of Clarkson N. Potter, Inc.

Printed in China

Design by Rita Marshall with Lisa Sloane

Library of Congress Cataloging-in-Publication Data is available upon request.

ISBN 0-517-70356-4

10 9 8 7 6 5 4 3 2 1

First Edition

A C K N O W L E D G M E N T S

This book would not have been possible without the invaluable assistance of all the men and women at Steinway & Sons. Among them are Warren Albrecht, Peter Goodrich, Frank Mazurco, Michael Mohr (and his father, Franz), Leo Spellman, Bruce Stevens, Bill Strong, and Bill Youse. A number of their suppliers were also very kind with their time and generous with their knowledge: at the American Felt Company, Richard Ryan and Bryan Paschall; at O. S. Kelly, Russ Alberson, Clarence Bunch, Michael Conley, Jimmy Daniels, Michael Heironimus, Michael Pennywitt, Ken Peter, and Jerry Wilcox.

In addition, I would like to thank Henry Grossman, photo chronicler of the New York cultural scene, for the use of his image of Franz Mohr; the Lincoln Center Library for the Performing Arts, for their collection; Vincent Dente and Carnegie Hall, for the image of the interior of the hall; The Rodgers and Hammerstein Organization and the estate of Irving Berlin for the use of "I Love a Piano"; and all the men and women who have helped chronicle the history of the firm, and the instrument, over the years, especially D. W. Fostle, Richard K. Lieberman, Aimee Kaplan, and all the people at the LaGuardia and Wagner Archives at the Fiorello H. LaGuardia Community College of the City University of New York. Special thanks to my uncle Henry Ziegler Steinway, without whose encouragement this project would never have happened.

Thanks also go to Rita Marshall, the book's designer. And, finally, Rodica Prato, whose elegant drawings illustrate the book, is not only a fine artist but a wonderfully warm collaborator. Bottomless thanks to her and her husband, Roland Caracostea.

CONTENTS

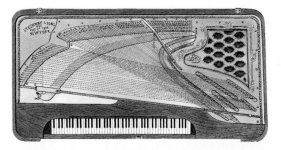

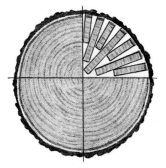
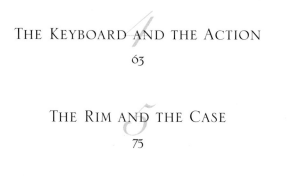
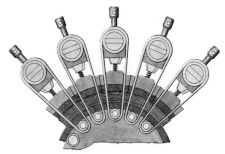

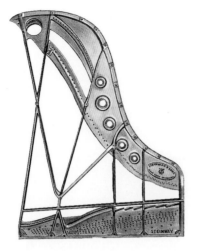

INTRODUCTION

About 150 years ago, my great-great-grandfather Henry Engelhard Steinway and his five sons formed a partnership to manufacture a musical instrument that was known at the time as the "pianoforte." In pragmatic German fashion they named their enterprise simply Steinway & Sons. These men and their descendants dedicated themselves to producing an instrument that would set the standard for quality. Their efforts rapidly paid off; within a short time of the company's founding in 1853, the family name, and their product, was famous throughout the world. Today, even though the company is no longer in family hands, the reputation of the instrument justifiably endures. The Steinway sits at the pinnacle of the piano maker's craft.

Pianos are strange creatures. Their shape is familiar, yet how many of us can say with any certainty what makes them work the way they do, why they are built the way they are, or what the difference is between a $50,000 grand and a $50 flea-market special? A Steinway grand piano has rightfully been called the most complex piece of machinery made by hand in the world today. The name alone is celebrated: "Steinway," in some quarters, means "piano," just as "Band-Aid" refers to the adhesive strip sold by the Johnson & Johnson Company.

I grew up in an environment where music was a way of life. A large black grand piano sat in a central position in our living room throughout my childhood. Many visitors to our home would sit down at that keyboard and produce sounds that amazed me when I was young—and the fact is, I'm still amazed. Although I don't play the piano myself, I have been fortunate enough to witness some great keyboard artists close at hand, and I have even been lucky enough to get to know a few of them. If I envy anything about those artists, it is their ability to make themselves at home at the keyboard (wherever they happen to find that keyboard) and communicate something wondrous in a manner beyond words. The passion of those artists, passion both for music and for the Steinway piano, has never left me.

Aside from its leading role as musical instrument, the piano has been thought of as furniture, decoration, prop, icon, and even investment. Yet in reality, pianos are intensely sophisticated machines, the product of highly refined engineering, design, and craft. At Steinway & Sons they are also part of an ongoing history—and they are made basically the same way they were a hundred years ago. The firm's dedication to quality is still very much present, as is what my grandfather Theodore Edwin Steinway once termed the family's sense of "service to music."

In the past half-century, the piano has undergone little change, but the piano business has changed considerably. Competition from other sources of home entertainment, such as radio, television, sophisticated stereo equipment, and computers, has taken a toll, and competition from other keyboard instruments, especially electronic ones, has placed the piano in an awkward marketing position. Few pianos are made in the United States anymore, and some companies can turn out as many pianos in a day as Steinway makes in a month.

This book will show you how a Steinway piano is made today at the New York City factory that is home to Steinway & Sons' American operation. Visitors to the factory are always impressed by the completeness of the operation, with stacks of lumber curing in the open air at one end and a loading dock shipping out finely finished instruments at the other. Over five hundred people are involved in the process, and it can take several years to make one piano. The process involves the disciplines of mechanical engineering, design, wood technology, carpentry, cabinetmaking, wood finishing, metallurgy, and a nearly miraculous step called voicing. The missing element here is music: you will have to supply that yourself. So put on a favorite record or compact disc, and take a journey from the prosaic to the poetic as we give you the keys to piano making, behind the walls at the Steinway & Sons factory.

*"Giraffonflügel," highly decorated giraffe piano
by Josef Wachtl, Vienna, c. 1817*

*Upright grand piano by Muzio Clementi & Co.,
London, 1816*

*Pyramid piano by Leopold Sauer,
Prague, c. 1805*

*Marie Antoinette's square piano, by Erard,
Paris, 1787*

*"Sewing Box" piano, maker unknown,
southern Germany, c. 1805*

A Brief History of the Instrument and Its Makers

Giraffe piano, maker unknown, probably Vienna, c. 1835

HAMMER DULCIMER

THE EARLIEST ANCESTOR of the modern piano is generally considered to be the instrument described in a 1700 inventory of the Florentine court as an *arpicembalo che fà il piano e il forte* (literally, the "harpsichord that can play quietly and loudly") and credited to Bartolomeo Cristofori, a Paduan harpsichord builder in the employ of a Medici prince. Searching for a way to increase both the volume of sound that could be produced and the keyboard's response to the musician's touch, Cristofori made a cru-

1700
Bartolomeo Cristofori invents the pianoforte

1703
Peter the Great founds St. Petersburg

1715
Louis XIV dies in France

1727
Diamonds are discovered in Brazil

1701
Detroit is founded in North America

1707
England and Scotland united as Great Britain

1721
J. S. Bach composes Brandenburg Concerti

cial modification in his instrument's action by devising a mechanism that struck the strings with variable force, depending on the amount of pressure placed upon the keys, and then withdrew so the note could be repeated rapidly. Inadvertently, Cristofori had "invented" the instrument we now call a piano.

There are only a few methods by which the strings in any instrument can be excited, or set to vibrate, thereby making sound. They can be bowed (as in a violin, cello, or any member of that family), plucked (as in a guitar, harp, or zither), or struck by an object. Before Cristofori's invention, the only keyboard instrument in which the strings were struck to produce sound was the clavichord, but the piano's story more properly begins with another stringed instrument, the hammer dulcimer.

Dulcimers, monochords, lyres, and the like are among the oldest stringed instruments on the planet. What would our image of the ancient Greeks be without a lyre? (This symbol of antiquity is even reflected in the Steinway & Sons emblem.) These types of simple instruments are found all over the world, in many different forms. The hammered dulcimer, a stringed box laid in the lap and played with two beaters, was known in the Middle East in the early Middle Ages. In Germany during the 1600s, the hammer dulcimer was called a *hackbrett,* or "butcher block," which demonstrates the level of regard in which the instrument was held. In the early 1700s the instrument gained new respect when an itinerant dancing master from Leipzig with the unwieldy name of Pantaleon Hebenstreit created a sensation in the royal courts of northern Europe playing a custom-made hammer dulcimer of gigantic proportions.

1731
Bach composes Six Partitas

1742
Bach composes Goldberg Variations

c. 1750
"Baroque" era ends; "Classical" era begins

1756
Wolfgang Amadeus Mozart born in Salzburg

1736
Natural rubber is discovered in Peru

1750
Bach dies in Leipzig at age 55

1754
French and Indian War begins

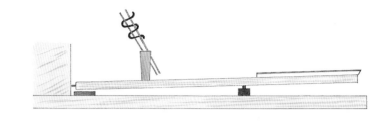

Hebenstreit's dulcimer, which by 1697 was known simply as the Pantaleon in honor of its virtuoso, was a massive beast. Nine feet long, it sat upon its own legs and had 186 metal strings. Hebenstreit either sat at or stood over it. The strings were hit with a downward stroke from a wooden mallet as long as a modern drumstick, although the size and exact construction have never been determined. The mallets were probably covered with leather at the business end, possibly faced with a softer material on the underside. There was no easy way to dampen the strings' vibrations, so the instrument produced a rolling, ringing sound. Trills and arpeggios would hover in the air, seemingly forever. Because the instrument lacked dampers, the unstruck strings resonated with sympathetic vibrations, producing overtones that added harmonics to the notes. Hebenstreit could

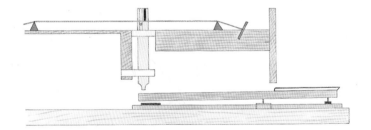

vary the sound of his dulcimer to a degree unheard of in those days: by exciting the strings at different points along the length of the instrument, by varying the force of his blows, by using the hard or soft sides of his mallets, or by a combination of all three.

The effect on his listeners was electrifying. Royal audiences and common folk

1757
Domenico Scarlatti dies

1763
France cedes control of Canada to England

1768
First piano concert in England, by Johann Christian Bach

1778
Mozart composes Turkish Sonata

1762
Catherine the Great crowned empress of Russia

1767
Charles III banishes Jesuits from Spain

1776
Declaration of Independence signed

alike became intoxicated with the sound Hebenstreit could produce, and he became the musical superstar of his day. His success was due partly to the spectacular image he presented (imagine a man hunched over his monster instrument, flailing away with mallets and creating a cascade of sound unlike anything that had been heard before), but what really impressed listeners was the *variety* of sounds that Hebenstreit produced. He could play loud or soft, forcefully or gently, fast or slow. The range of expression he could coax out of his instrument was astonishing, and Hebenstreit's successes, both popular and imperial, did not go unnoticed by the musicians or the instrument makers of the day. This musical phenomenon set off a frenzy of design—to adapt the physics of

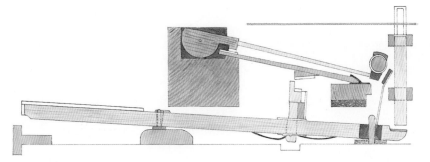

Cristofori adapted the physics of the hammer dulcimer to the keyboard.

the hammer dulcimer to the keyboard instrument. Cristofori, although probably never having heard Hebenstreit play, anticipated this development by a few short years.

The clavichord, in use by the fifteenth century, also employs a striking mechanism to produce sound, but the volume is softer, more intimate, and better suited to the chamber than the concert hall. In a clavichord, the strings are struck by a metal rod, known as a tangent, which is mounted directly on the key at the end opposite the player. When the key is pressed down, the tangent rises to strike the string, at once activating the vibration and determining its "speaking" length. The speaking length of the string,

1783
U.S. independence recognized

1786
Mozart composes Concerto in C minor

1789
Revolution begins in France

1795
Toussaint L'Ouverture takes control of Haiti

1785
Mozart composes Concerto in D major

1788
Mozart composes Coronation Concerto

1791
Mozart dies in Vienna at age 35

along with its tension, determines pitch, be it a C-sharp or B-flat or another note. When the finger pressure on a clavichord's key is released, the tangent falls and the vibration is dampened by a piece of cloth, called a listing, which rests upon one end of the string. The sound of a clavichord is somewhat responsive to the player's touch, but other factors limit the instrument's expressiveness. Trills, for example, are nearly impossible to play on a clavichord, since two keys often strike the same string at different speaking lengths to create two different notes. Despite the fact that the clavichord was the most expressive keyboard instrument of its day and a favorite of the era's composers (J. S. Bach is said to have preferred it to any other keyboard instrument, save the pipe organ, and wrote his *Well-Tempered Clavier* for it), it was, and is still considered to be, a specialty instrument.

Without a doubt the most popular stringed keyboard instrument in Cristofori's time, and the one most in use, was the harpsichord. Until the general acceptance of the pianoforte, the harpsichord was deemed the premier keyboard instrument for both solo and orchestral work. Like the clavichord's tangent, the harpsichord's jack (the activator that touches the strings) lies directly upon the instrument's key, with no mechanical interface between it and the musician. Unlike the clavichord, the harpsichord works by a plucking rather than striking mechanism. Its simple action results in a fuller sound, but one that cannot, unfortunately, be modified to any great degree in timbre or volume by the player's touch. Variation in a harpsichord's sound is achieved by other factors: by applying and releasing dampers, by plucking or not plucking alternate sets of stings, and by simply opening or closing the top of the case.

In attempting to combine the expressive characteristics of an instrument such

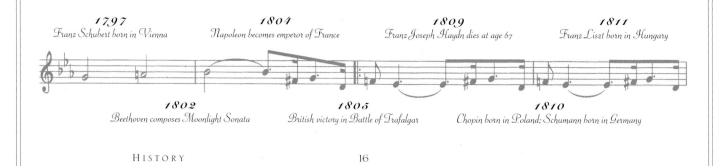

1797
Franz Schubert born in Vienna

1804
Napoleon becomes emperor of France

1809
Franz Joseph Haydn dies at age 67

1811
Franz Liszt born in Hungary

1802
Beethoven composes Moonlight Sonata

1805
British victory in Battle of Trafalgar

1810
Chopin born in Poland; Schumann born in Germany

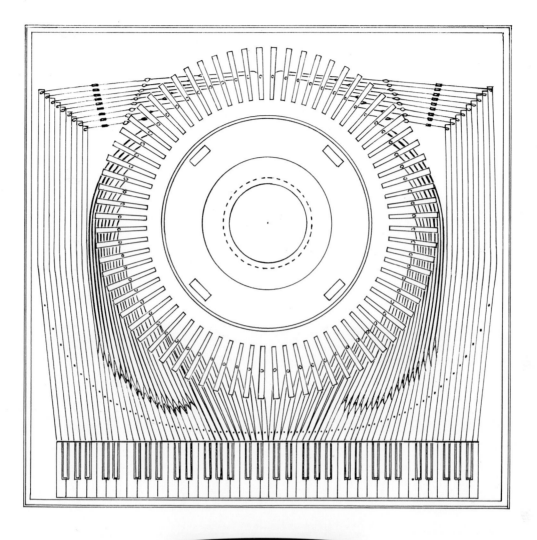

ROUND PIANO

Schematic diagram for round piano (never constructed),

French, c. 1780.

SQUARE PIANO

A Steinway square piano c. 1888. Most of the pianos made for home use at that time were square.

1829
Schubert dies at age 31

1832
Chopin makes Paris debut

1839
Schumann premieres Schubert's Symphony #5

1841
Chopin composes Fantaisie in F minor

1831
Charles Darwin sets out on 5-year Pacific voyage

1836
Henry E. Steinway completes his first piano

1840
Liszt gives solo piano "Recital" in London

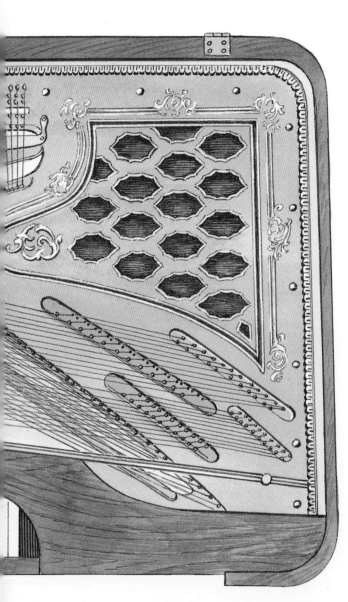

as the Pantaleon with the convenience and the chord-playing ability of the keyboard, instrument builders came to many technological dead ends over the course of a century. Independent of Cristofori and of each other, the Frenchman Jean Marius and the German Gottlieb Schröter had carried out preliminary work on the problem, but neither could find financial backing. In 1726 another German, Gottfried Silbermann, having seen an account of the Cristofori mechanism, and aware of his contemporaries' efforts, set about producing a similar instrument in his own workshop. By the late 1700s, as Silbermann's former employees spread out across Europe and began building their own instruments, two basic designs for the "pianoforte," as the new instrument was called, had emerged: the Viennese and the English. The differences between the Viennese and English actions were technical, but they led to furious competition between makers of pianofortes derived from the two layouts. In London, Paris, Vienna, and many points in between, competing instrument makers would often denigrate one another's products, but these rivalries did not hinder the pianoforte from becoming a favorite of composer and audience alike by the year 1800. By then the

1845
Schumann composes Piano Concerto in A minor

1849
Chopin dies in Paris at age 39

1852
Napoleon III made emperor of France

1854
Steinway & Sons factory opens in New York

1848
Gold discovered at Sutter's Mill, California

1850
Steinway family arrives in U.S.

1853
Commodore Perry arrives in Japan

Americans were also making pianofortes, but most of the technical progress, along with the greater part of the market, was in Europe. It wasn't until the middle of the nineteenth century that American pianos became known on the world stage.

Since the piano incorporates highly sophisticated engineering in its design, the radical changes wrought by the Industrial Revolution had their own profound effect on the development of the instrument. These changes manifested themselves in ways that had implications not only for pianos, but for pianists and for piano companies as well. Concert halls became larger, for example, and audiences grew far beyond the boundaries of the royal courts. Bigger halls necessitated louder instruments, and the newer music required more expressive ones. A middle class, with money and leisure time, emerged. All of these things influenced the design, marketing, and manufacturing of the piano during the nineteenth century.

Before 1800, the use of metal inside the instrument, except for strings and fasteners, was practically unheard of, but by midcentury iron began to supplant wood as a structural material, thereby allowing greater string tension and an increased "dynamic range" of volume. Makers also started using metal in the action of the piano, which permitted easy regulation for evenness of touch and afforded resistance to the vicissitudes of climatic conditions. Each modification was driven by the desire to create an instrument with a bigger sound, greater durability, and increased flexibility for the keyboard artist.

As in other industries, the forces of capitalism unleashed an unbridled desire for profit, which also spurred invention. As railroads, steamships, and communication technologies began to make the world a smaller place for business, new opportunities opened up for enterprising merchants. Western music followed the empire builders,

1855
Steinway wins gold medal at American Institute Fair

1857
First passenger elevator in New York

1859
Henry Steinway, Jr., patents overstrung grand piano

1861
Civil War starts

1856
Schumann dies in Germany at age 46

1858
Camille Saint-Saëns appointed organist at La Madeleine church, Paris

1860
Second Steinway factory opens on 53rd and Park

and soon piano makers had a larger international market for their instruments, to which they happily offered a range of new and distinctive models. The expressiveness of the instrument increased, and music written for the piano evolved to take advantage

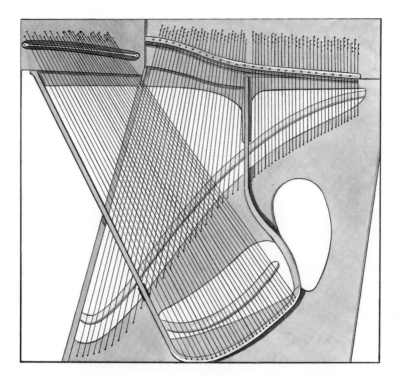

The harp and strings of the vertical, or "upright," piano around the turn of the twentieth century.

of it. The Classical repertoire yielded to the Romantic, and the phenomenon of the key-board virtuoso followed quickly behind. Now the musician, who was often the composer as well, had more control over the sound, and the music fell upon a greater number of ears. A concert tour took these newfound darlings of the public imagination to places that may never have seen a professional musician before. Home entertainment, an invention of the Victorian era, put pianos in the parlor in addition to on the concert stage. The demand for instruments was unprecedented, and they came in many

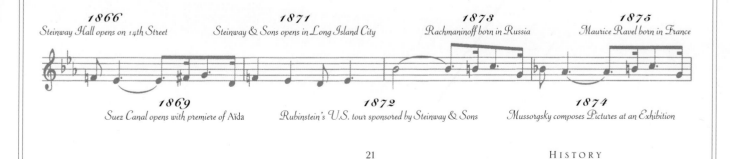

1866
Steinway Hall opens on 14th Street

1871
Steinway & Sons opens in Long Island City

1873
Rachmaninoff born in Russia

1875
Maurice Ravel born in France

1869
Suez Canal opens with premiere of Aïda

1872
Rubinstein's U.S. tour sponsored by Steinway & Sons

1874
Mussorgsky composes Pictures at an Exhibition

shapes and sizes: round, square, triangular, curved, vertical, and horizontal. Society was changing rapidly, and the numbers of manufacturers of pianos (the name "pianoforte" fell out of general use by 1900) exploded as the middle class grew. Pianos became big business.

Lyre piano,

maker unknown,

probably Berlin,

c. 1825.

The Industrial Age was punctuated by the great international expositions, and in 1867, in Paris, an American piano manufactured by the recently founded firm of Steinway & Sons surpassed the instruments shown by the French, English, German,

1876
Alexander Graham Bell invents telephone

1880
Steinway & Sons factory opens in Hamburg

1886
Liszt dies in Bavaria at age 75

1877
First music demo transmitted by wire, at Steinway Hall

1882
Debussy composes Claire de Lune

1891
Paderewski's U.S. tour sponsored by Steinway & Sons

Viennese, and other American manufacturers and won first prize. It was the first time an American manufacturer had done so. This instrument featured several innovations that provided greater response to the musician's touch and a bigger, more brilliant sound across the entire keyboard than had ever been heard before. It announced the

"Janko" keyboard upright piano, Decker Brothers, New York, 1892.

arrival of a new piano manufacturer on the international scene and secured the reputation that the company enjoys to this day. This piano's design, which incorporated a one-piece, overstrung iron frame within a solid bentwood frame, came to be known as

1892
Rachmaninoff wins gold medal, Moscow Conservatory

1897
Brahms dies at age 64

1903
Steinway & Sons presents piano #100,000 to T. Roosevelt

1908
Prokofiev publishes Piano Sonata #1

1895
Marconi invents radio

1901
Rachmaninoff premieres Piano Concerto #2

1906
Aleksandr Scriabin makes U.S. debut

the Steinway System, and it was thoroughly scrutinized by the other manufacturers. It soon supplanted the instruments offered by the European manufacturers, and within a few years' time many of its features became the standard of the industry.

Henry Engelhard Steinway, born Heinrich Engelhardt Steinweg in 1797, made his first pianos in the family's home in the Harz mountains of southern Germany. Regional politics were tumultuous and bloody at the time, and Henry wished for a stabler environment, economically as well as politically, in which to build his pianos and raise his family of twelve. In 1849 his second-oldest son, Charles, who had recently journeyed to the United States, reported that New York was the place to be, and he urged the family to join him there. New York, said Charles, offered a burgeoning German-American community, numerous piano factories where hardworking German-speaking men could be employed, and no military draft. This must have been the news that Henry was waiting to hear. He took some time to settle his affairs, then packed up almost the entire family and booked passage to the United States. Henry; his wife, Julianne; and their children (one daughter had died in infancy, and a son died soon after their arrival) landed in New York on June 9, 1850.

One son, the oldest, C. F. Theodore, remained in Germany, where he continued his experiments in design and continued to build pianos. Although separated by an ocean from the rest of the family for many of the coming years, C. F. Theodore would nonetheless become an essential part of the firm. An engineer by training and an iconoclast by disposition, he was responsible for many of the patents that assured Steinway

Steinway patented the Hexagrip Pinblock in 1963. The alternating forces of seven laminations of wood grain hold the tuning pin securely.

1909
Rachmaninoff makes U.S. debut

1913
Stravinsky's Rite of Spring premieres in Paris

1915
Scriabin dies at age 43

1918
Debussy dies in Paris at age 56

1911
Ravel composes Valses Nobles et Sentimentals

1914
World War I begins

1917
Revolution in Russia

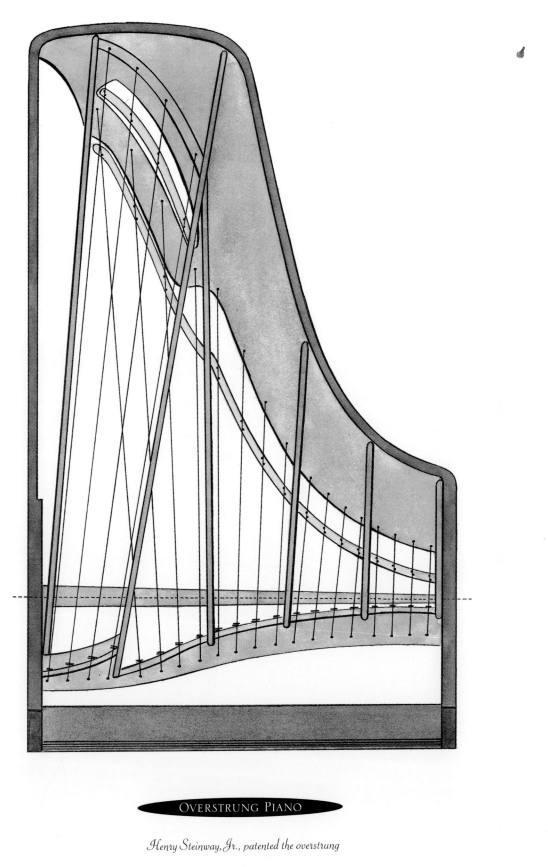

OVERSTRUNG PIANO

Henry Steinway, Jr., patented the overstrung

grand-piano frame in 1859.

THE STEINWAY FAMILY

of technological supremacy. His experiments created a new "scale" for the Steinway piano and a new sound for the instrument. Many of C. F. Theodore's innovations have not been surpassed to this day.

The newly Americanized Steinway family settled into their new home at 199 Hester Street on the Lower East Side in Manhattan. New York was a bustling center of manufacturing at that time—there were over thirty piano manufacturers in Manhattan alone—so Henry and his sons who were old enough found work at several different piano factories. Despite the fact that he never learned to speak English and could not read or write, Henry went to work for the firm of Lighte, Newton & Bradbury, building soundboards for $6 a week. Henry Jr. made a dollar a week more building keyboards for James Pirsson, who played the double bass in the young New York Philharmonic Orchestra and built pianos in his spare time. Two other sons, the aforementioned Charles and the fourth-oldest son, William, worked for another manufacturer, William Nunns, whose company was soon liquidated (William Steinway was owed $300, representing eight months of working six days a week, twelve hours a day, and never collected) and merged to become the well-known firm of Nunns & Clark. The youngest son, Albert, stayed at home, as did the three daughters.

Three years later the Steinway men had achieved enough success to leave their various employers and make an informal agreement among themselves to build their own pianos. In 1853 the firm of Steinway & Sons was born. Incorporation papers followed a few years later.

1920
League of Nations founded

1924
Gershwin's Rhapsody in Blue premieres

1928
Ravel makes U.S. debut in Boston

1933
Steinway Street subway station opens in Queens

1921
Saint-Saëns dies in Algiers at age 86

1925
Second Steinway Hall opens on 57th Street

1929
Stock markets crash, leading to Great Depression

The first American Steinway pianos were actually built where the family lived on Hester Street, but it is unclear if they were sold under the Steinway name. Business was good enough, though, that they soon rented a loft at 85 Varick Street in Lower Manhattan and relocated the operation to what is considered to be the first Steinway & Sons factory. Within a year the Steinways took over an entire building nearby at 88 Walker Street, in the heart of what was then considered "piano row" in New York. There they created their first piano showroom. The whole family was involved—even one of Henry's daughters, Doretta, worked in the salesroom, and she occasionally offered free lessons to close a sale. Five years later the company moved to a brand-new factory building, uptown on what was then called Fourth Avenue. Today the street is called Park Avenue and the location is occupied by the Seagram Building.

The growth of the firm was so rapid, and the labor situation in Manhattan so intense, that by 1870 William Steinway began to purchase land for the company in the outer boroughs, on Bowery Bay in a part of New York that is now called Astoria, Queens. At first the location's use was limited to the lumber and iron operations, but it was not long before other departments were moved out of Manhattan. The family made a tidy profit when they sold the Fourth Avenue real estate, and the firm consolidated its manufacturing operations in Queens in the early years of the twentieth century.

Much of the early fame gained by the Steinways can be attributed to the company's supremacy during the great industrial expositions of the mid- to late nineteenth century. By 1862 the firm had won over thirty-five awards domestically for its instru-

1936
Civil War in Spain

1938
Steinway & Sons presents piano #300,000 to F. D. R.

1941
Ignacy Jan Paderewski dies at age 81

1947
Composer Charles Ives wins Pulitzer Prize

1937
Gershwin dies at age 39; Ravel dies at age 62

1939
Germany invades Poland

1943
Prokofiev composes Stalingrad Sonata

ments, but it was in Europe where the Steinways had their greatest success. After their first-prize win in Paris in 1867, there came a series of spectacular successes: in Vienna in 1873, at the Philadelphia Exposition of 1876, and in Chicago in 1893. Aside from the awards, however, what really set Steinway & Sons apart from the rest of the pack in the late 1800s was its ability to market its product.

It was the second generation of Steinways, who took over the reins of the company following Henry Sr.'s death in 1871, who possessed the business acumen. William, who headed the firm until his own death in 1896, was primarily responsible. He was fourteen when the family arrived in New York, an age that makes him de facto the first Americanized Steinway: he spoke both English and German fluently. Gifted with business sense as well as piano-making skills, William was the first to realize that to sell pianos one needed to sell something else, something larger: an image of refinement, of grace, of civilized culture, and even music itself. In short, he recognized that before one is a piano buyer, one must first become a music lover. And so to engender a love of music in the populace, he brought several of the leading keyboard artists of the day to the United States and promoted national concert tours, which he launched from New York's own Steinway Hall. Anton Rubinstein, a superstar in his day, was the first, and William kept him busy touring for more than a year, starting in 1872. Ignac Jan Paderewski, another artist with a romantic, highly devoted following, began his thirty-year association with the firm in 1891. Josef Hofmann and Sergei Rachmaninoff soon followed. Soliciting the great musicians' testimonials for use in company advertising, William eventually made the Steinway name familiar to all.

By the year 1900, the firm of Steinway & Sons was world renowned. There

1948
State of Israel founded

1957
Jean Sibelius dies in Finland at age 92

1961
Yuri Gagarin becomes first person in space

1967
First successful heart transplant, in South Africa

1953
Korean War ends

1960
First laser constructed by Maiman in U.S.

1962
Cuban missile crisis

THE FIRST STEINWAY GRAND

SEESEN, GERMANY

S.S. *HELENE SLOMAN*

WALKER STREET FACTORY

STEINWAY PIANOS

AGE DEPOT

PIANOS

4TH (PARK) AVENUE FACTORY

FIRST HAMBURG FACTORY

DAIMLER ENGINE

USAF GLIDER

STEINWAY MOTOR LAUNCH

FIRST STEINWAY HALL

STEINWAY'S PIANOS

PIANO #100,000

DAIMLER MOTOR CARRIAGE

PIANO #300,000

STEINWAY MANSION

FERRY BOAT *STEINWAY*

THE CITY OF NEW YORK

BLACKWELL'S ISLAND

WARD'S ISLAND

RAVENSWOOD

JACKSON AVENUE

LONG ISLAND CITY

ASTORIA

CALVARY CEMETERY

BOWERY BAY ROAD

SECOND STEINWAY HALL

TOWN OF NEWTOWN

LONG ISLAND SOUND

MASPETH

PIANO #500,000

LONG ISLAND CITY FACTORY

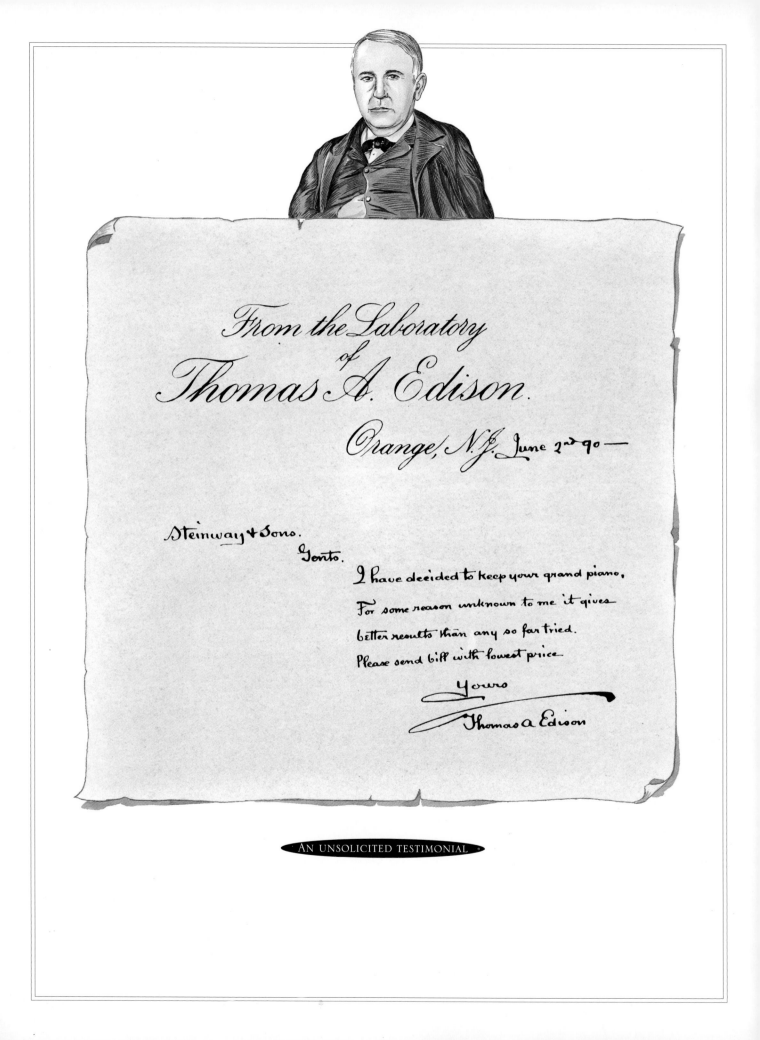

From the Laboratory
of
Thomas A. Edison.

Orange, N.J. June 2ᵈ 90 —

Steinway & Sons.
                Gents.

I have decided to keep your grand piano,
For some reason unknown to me it gives
better results than any so far tried.
Please send bill with lowest price

                Yours
                Thomas A. Edison

AN UNSOLICITED TESTIMONIAL

were two factories, in New York and in Hamburg, Germany; showrooms for the company's pianos in London, Hamburg, and New York; Steinway (concert) Halls in both London and New York; and a network of dealers with exclusive rights to the instrument throughout the world. There was an elite roster of "Steinway Artists," numbering among them just about every famous pianist alive, who publicly acknowledged the superiority of the instrument and played no other in concert appearances. Thanks to the N. W. Ayer Company and advertising copywriter Raymond Rubican, the Steinway piano came to be known as the "Instrument of the Immortals."

Steinway & Sons has been involved with numerous other ventures over the years, as shown in the drawing on the previous pages. Seesen, Germany, was the family's home. The boat that brought them to New York, the *Helene Sloman*, is pictured on the upper left. The ferryboat *Steinway* ran across the East River from the foot of 92nd Street. It brought pleasure seekers to the beaches of Bowery Bay, where the Steinways had extensive real estate holdings. The American rights to Gottlieb Daimler's 1891 internal combustion engine were held for a time by William Steinway; it powered yachts and motor cars he manufactured in Astoria. During World War II the New York factory built gliders for the U.S. Army. Five generations of Steinways, including two of my brothers, worked to ensure the lasting fame of the piano and to hold the quality of the instruments high. Through two World Wars, several economic depressions, the rise of mass-produced instruments, and the loss of most of the rest of the American piano industry, the Steinway name has remained at the very top. Although the family sold its financial interest in the firm in 1972, the sense of continuity and the care with which the pianos are made endure to this day.

1969
Americans land first man on moon

1972
Steinway family sells firm to CBS

1987
Steinway & Sons produces piano #500,000

1996
Selmer and Steinway merge

1971
Stravinsky dies in New York at age 89

1985
CBS sells Steinway & Sons to Steinway Musical Properties

1995
Steinway Musical Properties sells firm to Selmer Co.

HISTORY

Sugar Maple

Sugar Pine

Yellow Birch

C H A P T E R *2*

MATERIALS

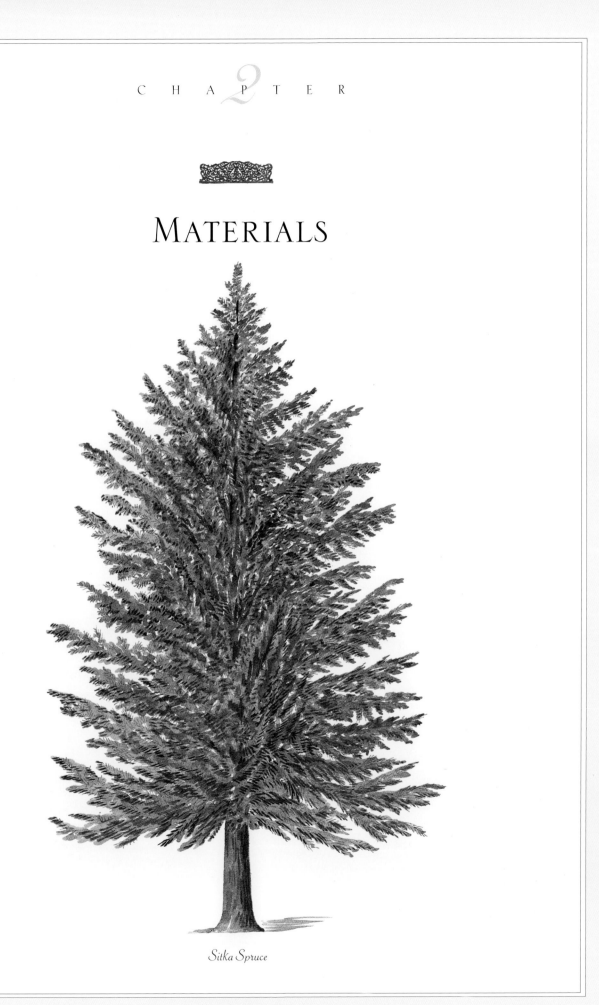

Sitka Spruce

THE FIRST THING visitors to the Steinway factory in New York see when they arrive is a vast lumberyard. This is fitting, because wood is the primary material used to make a piano. In order to keep the factory running at full speed, at least three months' supply must be available at all times, so at any given moment there is between $1.5 and $2 million worth of wood, some of it stacked neatly inside a large metal shed, but most of it carefully piled up in the open air. New, unskilled employees at Steinway & Sons often learn the trade working "in the lumber pile"; my uncles, who later ran the company, worked here when they started in the 1930s.

New York City is located at about 40 degrees latitude, around the same distance from the equator as Beijing, Rome, and Wellington, New Zealand. Consequently, the climate varies greatly throughout the year, which affects the woodpile just as it affects a finished piano. Hot, muggy summers alternate with freezing winters in New York, with more comfortable seasons in between. Through it all, the lumber sits quietly. Some people (bookkeepers especially) think it a waste to keep that much "inventory" lying around outside, but actually the wood is undergoing a crucial change: its moisture content is being reduced through evaporation. This natural aging is undeniably important if the finished product is to last. The wood spends anywhere from six months (for the lighter varieties) to over a year outside, and in some special cases longer than that, before it is taken inside the factory doors.

Wood is the main element in a piano, so in order to understand more about it, it is necessary to understand a few things about trees: how they grow, why one species is different from another, and how those differences are taken advantage of in the design and construction of a piano.

All trees share certain characteristics. For one thing, they grow taller only at the tips of their roots and at the terminal bud (called the apical meristem) where the leaves are. In between is what we call wood. As a tree grows, the limbs and trunk swell, and the layer just inside the protective bark, known as the cambium, produces new cells, but the bulk of the wood does not continue to grow. In a climate where the winters are cold enough to interrupt the growing cycle, such as in most of the United States, each year's growth of cambium is set down in a pattern of concentric rings, from which the age of a tree can be pinpointed with great accuracy.

The trunk is where nearly all the usable lumber is obtained, and it serves the tree in several ways. It offers support to the upper branches and limbs, and it carries nutrients and water from the leaves to the roots and back again. Seasonally, this trans-portation of nutrients (mostly sugars and proteins) and water works in one of two directions: upward toward the budding leaves for new growth in the spring, and downward for storage in the roots in midsummer, when the leaves are maximizing the production of sugars out of carbon dioxide from the air, sunlight, and water. This movement of water and nutrients takes place in a layer of wood just inside the cambium, known as the sapwood.

These dual functions of support and circulation continue throughout a tree's life, but the increasing mass of the limbs in a maturing tree necessitates a shift in emphasis as a tree gets bigger. In a budding shoot the primary goal is growth, but an older tree is obviously heavier than a young one, so the structural function becomes the priority. As this happens the main portion of the tree's trunk, the part that works solely as a means of support and does not carry fluid, turns into what is called the heartwood. Heartwood is considered physiologically inactive because its cells are dead and clogged with waste that gives the wood its characteristic color, depending on the species of tree. The pith, or core, lies at the very center of the trunk and is often where the natural rotting process begins.

It is the heartwood that is most useful for lumber. A cross section of a mature log reveals that the bulk of it is heartwood. Cut a tree too early, and you will get too much sapwood. Too late, and rot may have set in. Heartwood is also where most of the familiar visual characteristics of the wood type are revealed. For example, a log of

Lumber will warp to different shapes depending on where it was cut.

American black walnut (whose Latin name is *Juglans nigra*) shows a creamy color in its sapwood, and the familiar nut-brown cast only in the heartwood.

Most people acknowledge a basic difference in trees and lumber with the terms "hardwood" and "softwood," although the common use of these words is often misleading. A "hardwood floor" in a house, for example, may sometimes be covered with yellow pine (*Pinus echinata,* a name meaning "spiny pine"), which is a wood that botanists consider a softwood. The same thing is true with a lot of mass-produced furniture. The word "hardwood" in this case is used simply to specify that the item was

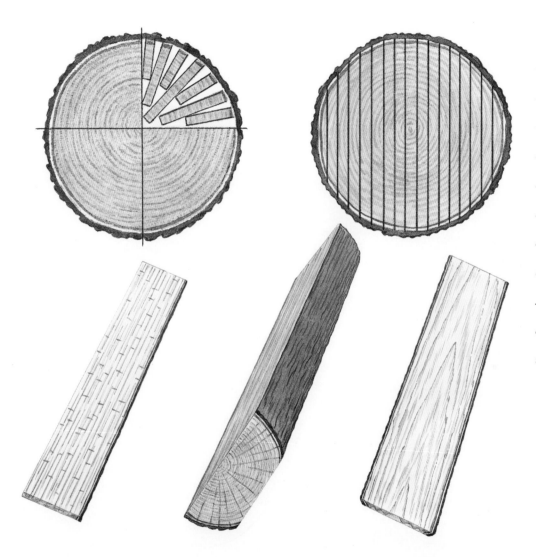

Quartersawn lumber (above and below left) results in the sturdiest boards. Plain-sawing (above and below right) produces more figuring in the wood. Both varieties can be cut from the same log (below center).

made from solid wood, not a composite of sawdust and resin covered with a wood-grain-type laminate. Furthermore, the very words themselves may be a bit misleading. There are hardwoods such as balsa (*Ochroma lagopus,* literally meaning "pale rabbit foot") that are much softer than a softwood such as Douglas fir (*Pseudotsuga menziesii,* a false hemlock named for the Scottish naturalist Archibald Menzies). Nor can one state with complete accuracy that conifers are softwoods and all other trees are hardwoods, although that is how the distinction is usually made.

The differences between hardwood and softwood have to do with the structure of the wood on a cellular level and with the origins of the tree's seed. It's quite complicated, but in general the common knowledge is correct: the softwoods are evergreens, while the hardwoods are broad-leaved trees whose leaves grow anew every year.

Like our own bodies, trees are mostly water, so freshly cut wood has a high moisture content. Some of the rough lumber at the Steinway factory is as much as 80 percent water by weight when it arrives. This has to be reduced, in a process called seasoning, to around 6 percent before the boards are worked. Air drying is the best, most natural method of ensuring even reduction of the wood's moisture content while retaining the highest degree of structural soundness. Although there are kilns that can accelerate the process, the slow, natural seasoning of the wood at the factory itself— each species at its own pace—is one of the distinguishing aspects of the manufacture of a Steinway piano. The kilns are used to give a final push to some recalcitrant types of lumber, and in a few cases to dry out a part that has just been glued—moisture from wet glue is absorbed by the wood and can sometimes cause it to swell.

As wood dries, a number of events occur that affect its usefulness. Small cracks, called checks, can form at the end grain of a board, but these are not really a problem, since checks and knots are cut out in the crosscut department, one of the first destinations for raw lumber inside the factory. Wood also tends to shrink as the water evaporates from it, which can cause a piece of lumber, or a finished part, to alter in size. This can be devastating in a finely machined part if the wood has not been properly seasoned to begin with, but it is not as important for dimension lumber at the beginning of the process. At this stage, the main problem to avoid is warpage. Again, if a board is going to be fashioned into a number of small parts, this might not in fact be a problem, and there are techniques in construction that help counteract warpage in the larger piano parts. There are also procedures in the milling process, which Steinway specifies to its suppliers, that can help minimize warpage at the outset.

By milling in what is known as a quartersawn process, lumber can be cut from a log in such a way so as to minimize warpage and add strength to the boards. Quartersawing is preferred for any application where strength is needed—fine furniture, flooring and decking, and the like—and where looks are to be considered, for it brings out more lustre in the wood. In this method the grain stays closely packed, no more than 45 degrees off vertical when viewed from the end of the board. Quartersawn boards are cut from the log radially, fanning out from the center. Milling lumber in this fashion is costly and creates more waste (there is little wood wasted at the factory, however; it is either resawn in smaller dimensions or burned for heat), but it creates the strongest boards. Quartersawn lumber is used for most of the structural pieces of a Steinway piano.

The beauty of the grain of a piece of wood can be brought out by a method called plain-sawing. Plain-sawn lumber is simply sliced lengthwise from a log, like slabs from the side of a sausage. Most of the veneers, the thin layers of wood that go on the outside surfaces of the piano, are solely decorative in function and are cut in this manner. As far as structural lumber goes, plain-sawing wastes little material but results in a collection of boards that can possibly warp a great deal or fail under pressure, depending on exactly where in the log they are cut. Because plain-sawing contributes to the looks of the material and usually not to its function, it is a technique that is employed by Steinway & Sons only when appropriate.

If you picture the end of a log as a clock face, the radially cut boards (the quartersawn boards) will come from the positions covered by the clock's hands when they are pointing at 12, 3, 6, and 9. A plain-sawn board would come from a line drawn through the numbers 11 and 7. Remembering that the tree's growth rings (which create

the wood's grain) circle the pith, you'll realize that the greatest number of rings, hence the greatest strength, will be found in the quartersawn boards.

A final word about grain. It is absolutely essential to have the correct grain in the wood for any piece that goes into a piano. The wood must be selected with great care, depending on the function of the piece. Vibrations, for example, travel along the grain very readily but not so easily across it. Wood also bends more easily along the grain but tends to split when the stress is delivered across it. Under compression, wood behaves in different ways depending on the application of stress in relation to the grain.

In terms of finishing (that is, the application of a finish to the wood), there are also differences in wood types. Some varieties, such as maple and birch, have what is known as a closed-grained surface, which means that the pores of the wood exposed by cutting are relatively small, nearly invisible to the naked eye. Closed-grained woods accept a built-up finish, such as varnish, more readily than do open-grained varieties because liquids tend to stay on the surface rather than penetrate into the wood. Before a built-up finish can be applied to an open-grained wood, the wood must first be treated with a sealer to fill the pores.

There are five main varieties of wood that go into a Steinway piano: birch, maple, sugar pine, poplar, and spruce. These woods are found in all the instruments the company makes, regardless of the model, color, or finish of the piano. Each has been found to have a unique suitability to the particular task it performs.

The birch is mostly **yellow birch** (*Betula alleghaniensis*, the species name of which means "of the Allegheny Mountains"), and the greater part of it comes

from the New England states and eastern Canada, although the tree naturally ranges from the Great Lakes south to North Carolina. Birch is a hardwood—very strong and durable, with an ability to accept a finish well. It is machined easily, as the grain is especially close and even textured, and has a natural cream to pale brown color. Because of its hardness, birch is used for the cores of the piano's hammers, but its workability makes it suitable for carved parts, such as the legs and pedal lyre, as well.

Several grades of maple are used at Steinway, but they all come from the same tree, the **sugar maple** (*Acer saccharum*), which is the tree that yields sweet maple syrup from its boiled-down sap. There are over twenty different varieties of sugar maple in the United States, and it is one of our most valued trees. Sugar maple is the state tree of four states and grows throughout most of the country east of the Rocky Mountains and on the northern Pacific coast. Because it is both durable and hard, it can be machined to

fine tolerances. Maple can also be exquisitely figured, meaning that it can contain beautiful grain patterns such as in the fiddleback and bird's-eye varieties, but in pianos it is used mostly for its physical properties rather than its looks.

The "action" maple, used to fabricate the small parts in the piano's action, must be all white and straight grained and comes from the Adirondack Mountains, Canada, and the New England states. The "wrestplank" maple, used in the block that holds the tuning pins, can be more yellowed and comes from a single mill in Vermont. This grade is rarer, as it must be knot-free for its entire length. Maple is also the principal wood in the piano's rim and case.

Sugar pine (*Pinus lambertiana*, named for Aylmer Bourke Lambert, an English pine specialist), a softwood, comes from one of the largest families of tree species in the world. This variety is one of the biggest true pines—some specimens have reached a height of 240 feet (four-fifths of a football field) and 18 feet in diameter. It is also known as the great pine, and it grows in mountainous areas of the Pacific drainage, from Oregon to Mexico. Sugar pine is considered  one of the finest of all pines for woodworking because it has consistent grain and shrinks and warps very little for a softwood. It is used for the ribs beneath a piano's soundboard, which add strength without a great deal of weight.

Yellow poplar (*Liriodendron tulipifera*), also called the tulip tree, should not be confused with the exotic Brazilian hardwood known as the tulip tree. Yellow poplar is one of the most useful and valuable hardwoods in the United States—and the state tree of three states—but it is practically unknown to the average person. Try asking for poplar at your local lumberyard—they may stock the odd board or two, but it is used more often in industry rather than by home craftspeople. Poplar grows in moist areas  throughout eastern North America, as far north as southern Canada. Its flowers are especially sweet and fragrant, and their copious nectar produces a strongly flavored honey. The wood is of a green to yellowish cast, depending on if the tree is from a first- or second-growth forest. Poplar is used in furniture construction, for interior woodwork for houses, and, interestingly, for hat molds by the millinery trade. It does not absorb moisture easily and so is used as a "core" wood in

Opposite:

Steinway keeps

$1.5 to $2 million

inventory of

lumber on hand

in Long

Island City.

pianos, for panels and surfaces that are meant to be veneered, such as tops, keylids, and music desks. It has a fairly straight grain of even texture and is milled easily because it is relatively soft.

The most crucial element in the entire piano, the soundboard, is fashioned of **Sitka spruce** (*Picea sitchensis,* so named because it was first identified in the vicinity of Sitka, Alaska). Because the  soundboard has a very specific function in the instrument's performance, it's easy to list the desirable characteristics of its material: it must be light in weight but have a high modulus of elasticity. Or, in less technical terms, it must be able to withstand great down-bearing pressure from the strings and yet remain flexible enough to transmit their finest vibrations. Clear, evenly colored, straight-grained spruce with no fewer than ten growth rings per inch has been found to be the finest wood for this purpose. The sources of this timber have shrunk in recent years, and logging practices for it are hotly debated, especially since first-growth (or old-growth; that is, virgin) forests are the source of the best wood.

Sitka spruce trees grow in a narrowly bounded strip no more than 50 miles from the Pacific Ocean, in mountainous forests no higher than 3,000 feet, from northern California to Alaska. In these regions trees grow slowly and live long, so the wood has a tremendously dense and even grain for a softwood while retaining its characteristic lightness. Most of the trees that are being logged today come from the nearly inaccessible areas of their habitat, mostly hillsides, and the wood from these trees has a more variable grain structure. Consequently, the quality control for soundboard spruce at Steinway & Sons is very strict. Between only 1 and 2 percent of a standing tree is considered good enough to ship, and Steinway rejects about half of what it receives from its suppliers. The company's chief wood technician estimates that he spends

80 percent of his time in pursuit of soundboard spruce. The "holy grail" of piano makers (and guitar, violin, and other instrument makers as well) is a stable, renewable source for this timber. Sitka spruce is also used for pulp in paper making and was, in the early days of aviation, the preferred material for airplane construction.

For those of us who care about old forests, it seems somehow proper that if old-growth timber is to be harvested at all, it should end up with as glorious a task as that performed by a piano's soundboard.

Many exotic hardwoods are used to sheathe the Steinway & Sons instruments. Bubinga, cherry, ebony, bird's-eye maple, mahogany, rosewood, sapele, teak, and walnut are all available, and special orders can be obtained. Most of these exotic woods arrive at the factory in what is called a flitch, which is basically an entire section of tree trunk that has been plain-sawed into veneer. This method is different from rotary veneer cutting, in which a tree is spun against a fixed blade and comes off the log in sheets. Plain-sawn veneer is more difficult to obtain, and it costs more. Because a flitch contains a selection of veneer from a single tree, many decorative touches can be accomplished simply by arranging the pieces in different patterns. For example, a "book match" can create the image of a mask or a butterfly in the wood. This Rorschach-like quality of veneer is one of the marvels of fine woodwork, and it can be one of the most beautiful decorative elements in a Steinway. In any event, it is a mark of pride at the firm that every natural-finish piano contains veneers from only one individual tree.

The veneers have to be carefully selected and matched to show a consistent pattern throughout. This is a painstaking process, and the people who match the veneers, especially the smaller pieces (which are applied, for example, to the beveled edge of the piano's top), work with a patient and practiced eye that comes from years of dedication to their craft. It is fascinating to observe this veneer matching—sort of like watching a person assemble a jigsaw puzzle without peeking at the finished picture. A careful look at the case of any natural wood-finished Steinway will show you how good they are.

The choice of these particular wood varieties did not come about without experimentation. In 1862, for instance, Steinway & Sons purchased a large amount of "strictly quartered North Carolina mountain cypress," as my grandfather later termed it in a memoir, thinking that the wood would be suitable for soundboards. Since the swampy habitat of the cypress tree endows the wood with tremendous weather- and decay-resistant properties, the reasoning was that the material would prove superior to spruce. Alas, such was discovered not to be the case. With good German thriftiness, however, the stock was not wasted; a few years after their marriage my grandparents paneled a house with the remaining lumber, and my brother and his family live there today.

The oldest tool in the factory is a veneer cutter made in 1871. It is still in use today.

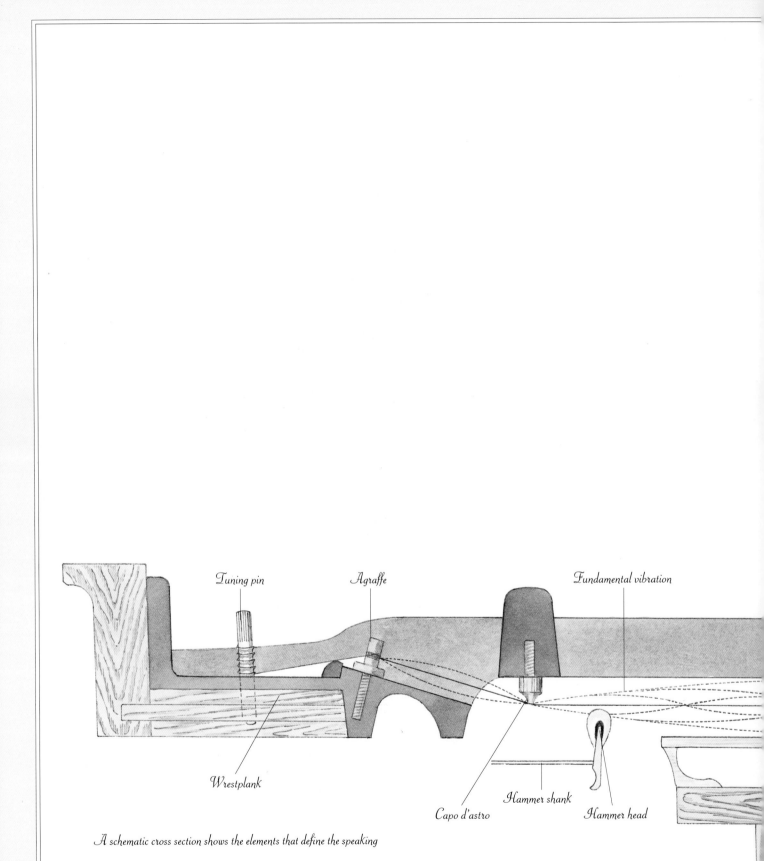

Tuning pin

Agraffe

Fundamental vibration

Wrestplank

Capo d'astro

Hammer shank

Hammer head

A schematic cross section shows the elements that define the speaking

length of the string. The dotted lines plot the string's vibrations.

The Soundboard, the Bridge, and the Physics of Sound

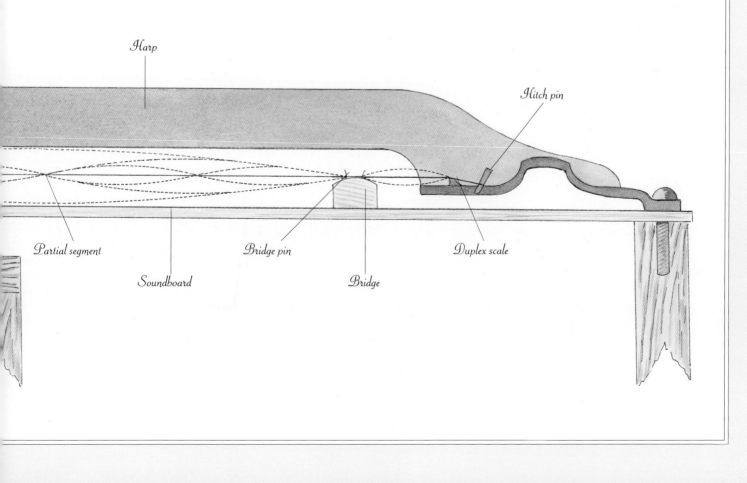

Harp

Hitch pin

Partial segment

Bridge pin

Duplex scale

Soundboard

Bridge

THE SOUND OF a Steinway piano has been compared to such diverse things as a thunderclap and a nightingale's song. But what defines the "Steinway Sound" is, in reality, tremendously subjective. Just as tastes in music have changed over the years, so too has the ideal of what a piano should sound like. Developments in piano design dovetailed with the evolution of music composition, yet the fundamentals of the production of sound by the instrument we call piano have not been radically altered since the instrument was first invented. A string is set to vibrate by a hammer's blow, sound is produced by the resulting vibrations, and the sound is amplified by a wooden diaphragm inside the instrument's case. Baby simple in theory, but infinitely complicated in practice.

It all starts with what is termed the "scale" of the piano. The scale, the basic layout of the insides of the instrument, is fundamental because it must produce the maximum amount of sound from the vibration of the strings. Every different-size piano will have strings of different lengths (the strings for a middle C on a 9-foot model D will be longer than the strings for the same note on a baby grand), so the scale of the piano must be designed to take into account each note, on each model. Moreover, every piano manufacturer has a proprietary set of scales for their instruments alone. These characteristic dimensions differentiate pianos from different makers more than any other technical element.

The soundboard and bridge of each Steinway model have a unique shape.

Model S

Model M

To be precise, for a particular piano, "scale" refers to the exact placement of all the interruptions along its strings' length, along with the exact point where the hammer strikes. In every piano the strings run from the tuning pins (just behind the keyboard) through the agraffes, or under the capo d'astro bar in the highest notes (which defines one end of the strings' speaking length); under the dampers (which hang above the point where the hammer hits); across the bridge (where the only physical contact is made between the string and the soundboard); and over a metal plate called the duplex scale (which constitutes the end of the speaking length of strings), finally terminating either by looping, or being tied off, around the hitch pins at the opposite end of the instrument. The distances between these interruptions must, by design, be set relative to two things: the overall length of the string, and the physics of a string's vibration. In the first case the instrument maker has nearly unlimited choice, but in the second he has none. Piano engineers have spent countless hours exercising their ingenuity trying to accommodate, compensate for, enhance, ignore, circumvent, attend to, and make peace with the laws of physics.

The scales used in Steinway & Sons pianos were developed primarily by C. F. Theodore Steinway in the second half of the nineteenth century, around the time of the introduction of the one-piece iron frame inside the piano. The iron frame made it possible to lengthen the bass strings by "overstringing" them, placing them above and crossing them over the treble

Model L

Model B

Model D

Soundboards are assembled from carefully matched spruce boards.

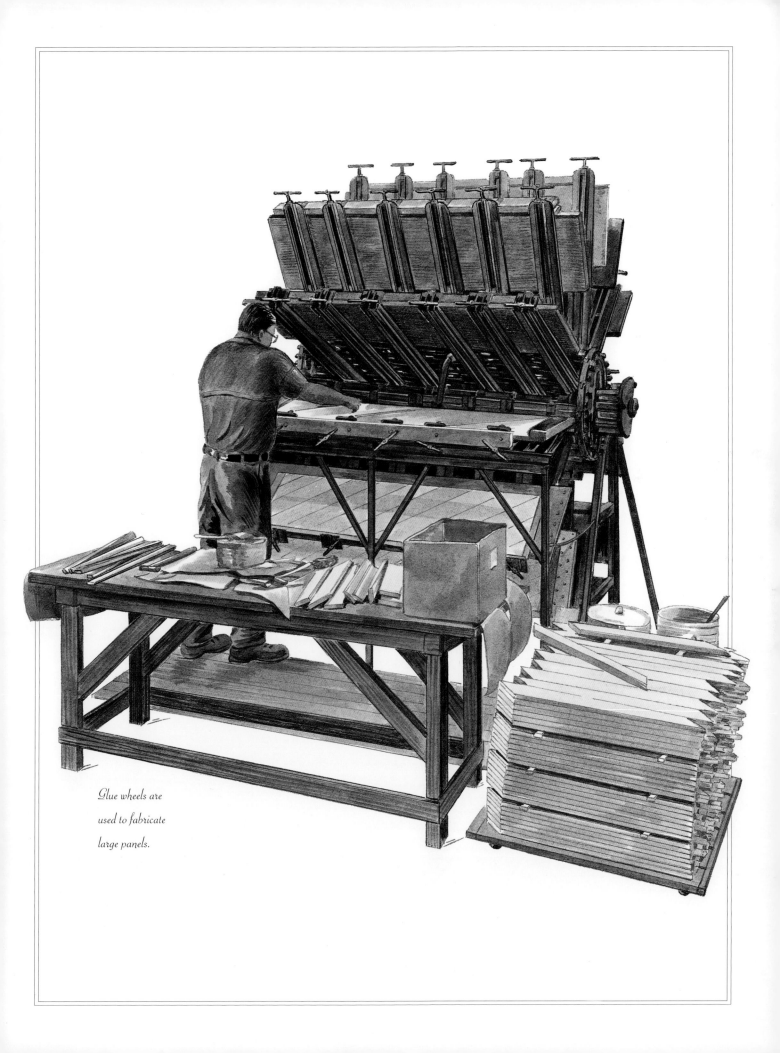

Glue wheels are
used to fabricate
large panels.

strings, which resulted in a richer sound coming from the same-size box. It also necessitated an adjustment to the shape of the bridge, which had been shaped in a graceful S curve before but now had to double-back on itself owing to the crossover. The bridge was also moved to a position closer to the center of the soundboard. These innovations resulted in greater volume and a richer, fuller tone.

So, too, did C. F. Theodore's patented "Duplex Scale." In this major leap, he reengineered the scale of the instrument to take advantage of what had previously been considered vibrational dead zones—beyond the speaking length of the string, between the bridge and the hitch pin. C. F. Theodore realized that if those areas of the string were sized correctly, they could enhance the piano's sound by vibrating in sympathy.

But what is it about a string's vibration that necessitates all the effort?

An excited string vibrates along its full length as one unit but also in *partial* segments, which result in overtones. These partials, and the harmonics they produce, form in a predictable series of divisions of the string's length. For example, the standard piano tuning is known as the 440-A. This means that the strings in the A above middle C are tightened until they vibrate 440 times a second along their full (speaking) length. At the same time, there are overtones produced from the partial vibrations of the strings' halves, thirds, quarters, fifths, and so on. The shorter, partial segments vibrate more rapidly than the fundamental one, so they produce higher pitches. The overtones rise in pitch in a mathematical sequence as the partial segment of the string gets shorter: 440 Hz (hertz, or vibrations per second), 880 Hz, 1,320 Hz, 1,760 Hz, and so forth. Most of these overtones are desirable (they give a fuller sound to the note), but many people consider overtones from the "dreaded" seventh and ninth harmonics upward to be disagreeable. It's a matter of taste, and of the physical limitations of the human ear. Generally speaking, higher partials are deemed acceptable in more contemporary music, such as the works of Arnold Schoenberg.

Production of the less desirable partials can be moderated to some extent by careful positioning of the location where the hammer strikes the string. If the string is excited close to a "node" (a demarcation point between like partials), this tends to reduce the vibration of that particular harmonic to some degree. As a result, the tone of the note varies considerably depending on where the string is hit. Because of this effect, a piano is usually constructed so that the hammers strike the strings somewhere between one-seventh and one-ninth of the distance from the beginning of their speaking length to the end, thus minimizing those particular harmonics.

This business of partials can be demonstrated easily with a guitar or any hand-held string instrument. Place your finger lightly on the exact middle of any string and pluck one side; you will hear a note even though your finger is damping the string's fundamental vibration. This is the first partial, or overtone, which comes from the vibrations of *half* the string. The other half of the string, the portion that was not excited directly, will vibrate *in sympathy*. Now pluck the whole string and look closely—you can see the vibrations of the string along its entire length, as well as the string's halves, quarters, and so on.

You can also demonstrate the effect of these partials on a grand piano. With the dampers lifted, pluck a string in the middle and you will hear a fundamentally warm, rich tone. If you pluck it near one of its ends, you will hear a different, thinner tone because the partial harmonics of the note have been excited to a greater degree. The point of contact between hammer and string is chosen to highlight the fundamental tone and the more pleasant sounding partials and to discourage the less pleasing ones.

The amount of sound produced by these partials, the time in which they individually rise and fall after the note is struck, and the total number of them that are audible when the note is held for a long period of time are what give a particular piano its characteristic sound. The differences between models, and between manufacturers, are audible even to those who lack a trained ear. Steinway pianos are known for their even tone along the full spectrum of sound and for their responsiveness to the pianist's

Bow Clamps

Wooden bow clamps, made of ash, hold the pine ribs

in place after they are glued to the soundboard.

demands—thunder in the bass and a clear high treble that can cut through the orchestra.

The scale of the piano is partly responsible for this, but you would not hear anything above a muffled "plink" if it weren't for the soundboard of a Steinway piano. The soundboard is constructed of carefully selected, quartersawn Sitka spruce boards laid up with the grain running parallel to the long edge of each board, because vibration travels along the grain of wood much better than across it. By the time the stock reaches the workbench, half of what the company has received from its suppliers has been rejected. There must be at least ten growth rings per inch in the wood, no knots, and an even color.

From the time the raw wood was delivered to the factory to the moment when an individual board is selected for a soundboard, the wood has been seasoned to the proper degree, the checked ends of the boards have been sawed off, the edges have been squared, and the boards have been machine-planed to a thickness of ½ inch, giving them the look of freshly cut lumber.

To construct a complete soundboard, a single worker first carefully selects the individual spruce boards, which can be of random width. He then places them side by side, matching them precisely to create a rough assembly. With a crayon, he next draws a semicircle across the entire surface, touching every piece. This ensures that if for some reason this collection of wood is disturbed, it can be reassembled and aligned properly in the match that the worker has given it. He then lowers a template that hangs above the workbench suspended by pulleys and trims the assemblage with an electric saw into a rough outline of the basic shape

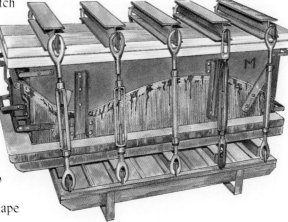

Each bridge is laminated from strips of maple and clamped into shape as the glue dries.

of the finished soundboard. When this is done, he stacks and bundles the boards.

Once a sufficient number of soundboards has been bundled, the boards are glued together, side by side, on a large rotating clamp, a glue wheel that resembles nothing so much as a huge office Rolodex (page 55). A different worker stands before the device and, after applying fresh glue to the edges of the boards that will butt up against one another, reassembles the panel on one of the flat surfaces that rotate around the center of the wheel. He then clamps the outer edges of the panel together gently— too much pressure, and the panel would pop out; too little, and the joints won't be tight enough—and rotates it up and away while the adhesive cures. A new gluing bed comes up from below, ready to accept the next soundboard.

Most of the large panels in the piano are also assembled on glue wheels. A number of other parts—keybeds and pedal lyres, for example—are also fabricated this way. Gluing up panels in this manner, from smaller pieces, is preferable to using fewer wide boards. This way, knots and small checks can be removed, and the grain of the individual pieces can be matched to add strength instead of weakening the panel. The joints between the boards add strength, too: the glue bond is actually stronger than wood.

The bridge, which is the only point of direct contact between the strings and the soundboard, is likewise made from several pieces of wood. Unlike in a panel such as a soundboard or top lid, however, the pieces of wood in a bridge are not glued together side by side but are bonded on top of one another ("laminated" is the proper word) in layers. The function of the bridge is to conduct vibration from the source (the strings) to the amplifier (the soundboard), so it must be rock solid. Bridges are made up from vertical strips of clear maple, topped horizontally with a single, thicker piece of the same wood. These strips are all laminated into a single piece and bent into their characteristic shape at the same time. The two largest models of grand pianos, the D and the B, have continuous, one-piece bridges; the other models have two-piece bridges. Each model's bridge, though, has a unique shape, so several different molds are used. Each mold looks and works differently but has the same function.

The bottom edge of each bridge is shaped to fit the crown of the soundboard. The crown, a domed shape that rises from the edges to the center of the soundboard, is crucial to the piano's sound. Like the back of a violin, the soundboard has to maintain this shape in order to amplify the sound of the strings' vibration to the greatest degree. Unlike the violin's back, however, a piano's soundboard is subject to tremendous downward pressure from many more strings held under greater tension, which has a natural tendency to flatten it. The crown must therefore be designed with that in mind, and it must be built into the soundboard as soon as practically possible.

A series of pine ribs, tapered at the ends and glued to the underside of the spruce panel, along with the curvature of the bottom of the bridge, secure the necessary shape of the panel. The soundboard-plus-ribs is then placed in a large freestanding press, which forces the assembly into shape during the first phase of its "double crowning." The second phase comes when the bridge, which has been precrowned on its bottom, is glued on. The ribs are attached at right angles to the grain of the spruce, so they also help disperse vibration across the full area of the soundboard.

Another important feature of the soundboard, and a Steinway patent since the 1930s, is the "Diaphragmatic" shape, a thinning of the perimeter of the soundboard, where it attaches to the rim of the piano, which enlarges the live area of the spruce panel and increases its potential to vibrate, and so maximizes the range of volume.

When you stand by a piano with a soundboard attached, but without the iron frame or strings, you begin to perceive the enormous potential of the instrument before you. The gleaming spruce (which has been given three coats of varnish) looks delicate, but if you slam your fist down on it (go ahead—it's constructed to withstand tremendous pressure), you hear a hollow "thwock" that echoes like a kettledrum.

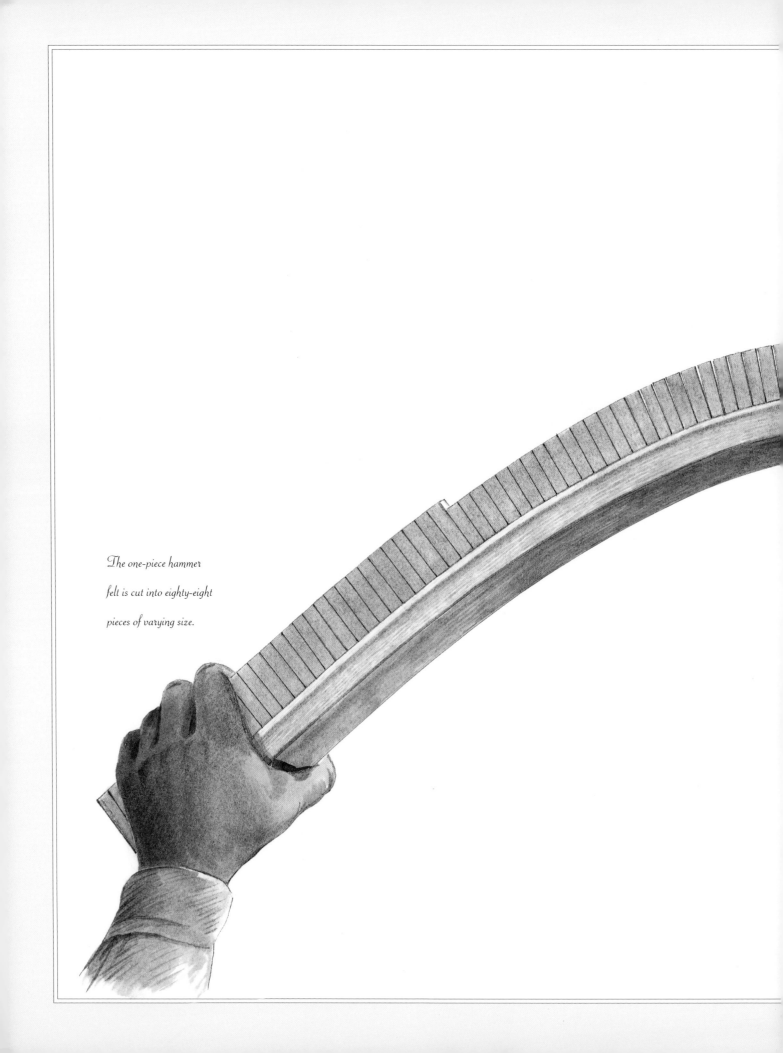

The one-piece hammer felt is cut into eighty-eight pieces of varying size.

The Keyboard
and the Action

PIANOS HAVE NOT ALWAYS had eighty-eight keys. What is known as the compass of the instrument—that is, the keyboard—has ranged from as few as four and one-third octaves, in Cristofori's time, to as many as ninety-seven keys in some models. This lengthening of the keyboard paralleled the composition of music in such a way that it is hard to determine which came first, the added notes to the piano or the composers' demand for them. At any rate, by the 1870s, around the time that Steinway & Sons had solidified its international reputation, a compass of eighty-eight keys spanning seven and one-quarter octaves was established as a standard.

The number of notes on the keyboard is far from the only matter on which piano manufacturers split opinion. Early on, for example, the design of the action was also the subject of debate. On one hand were proponents of the so-called Viennese style (just to make it more complicated, not all Viennese-style instruments were made in Vienna), in which the hammer heads face the keyboard and move away from the player when the keys are depressed. On the other was the English style (again, not all of these instruments were British in origin), in which the hammer heads are placed at the far end of the mechanism and move toward the player when the keys are struck. These different arrangements resulted in instruments that fell into two categories: the Viennese school produced more of a chamber-type instrument, while the devotees of the English action worked to achieve an instrument of greater dynamic range. A glimpse at any contemporary grand piano will show you that the

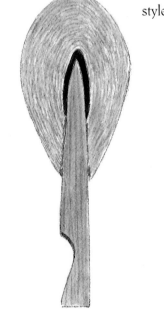

Side view of hammers from base and treble ends of the keyboard.

English model (which was Steinway & Sons' preference all along) has prevailed.

This choice was far from the only action-design problem facing piano makers. Some of them tried to duplicate the down-striking force of the hammer dulcimer in grand pianos, but the limitations of gravity proved too difficult to overcome. Others strove to improve the horizontal action, such as is found on vertical, or upright, pianos, which have never had the same feel as a grand. One enterprising Hungarian, Paul von Jankó, went so far as to redesign the entire keyboard as a series of six ranks of rounded knobs, replacing piano keys as we know them. His idea was to make learning

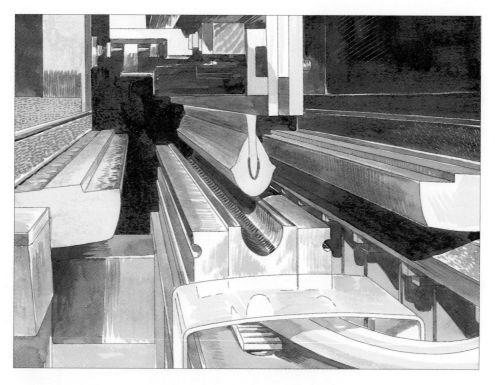

A copper mold presses the felt around the wood core to form all eighty-eight hammers at once.

to play the piano less difficult, because all the keys were the same height, and to improve the odds for people with small hands. Although a few piano makers did produce a number of instruments with this novel touch, it never caught on with the public. But no matter what path the designers and engineers followed, the basic function of the action and the requirements of its performance have remained consistent.

The action has to deliver a variable force to the string in such a way as to allow the note to be struck repeatedly in rapid succession, damping the vibrations between the notes each time unless the player wishes not to do so. It must remain noiseless and passive in the face of repeated attack from the keyboard artist but must give full, direct, and immediate response to the artist's ministrations. In other words, the action has to be able to articulate the delicate trills of an Art Tatum as easily as the pounding rhythms of a Little Richard. The touch of the key must also be easy enough to preclude fatigue to the pianist's muscles or ligament strain. Finally, the action must not break down under regular use, but it should be easy to service when the inevitable wear and tear does occur. Most of the mechanical engineering in piano design (in addition to the greatest number of parts in a piano) is found in the action. Servicing the action therefore must be simple, because each note has to be adjusted individually.

Cristofori's basic design has been refined by almost every piano manufacturer since his time, but there are two innovations that deserve special mention. The first is the "double repeating" action pioneered by the Frenchman Sébastian Érard in 1823, and the second is the "tubular metallic action frame" patented by C. F. Theodore Steinway in 1868. Érard's invention resulted in a significant increase in the expressive ability of the instrument, enabling the hammer to strike again before the key returned to its resting position. Steinway's invention contributed to the instrument's

Hammer   Hammer shank

Whippen   Tubular frame

durability—a consideration whose importance must not be discounted. In the late nineteenth century, keyboard virtuosos such as Franz Liszt always had several pianos on stage during concerts, in case one or more of them broke down. In Liszt's day some pianos literally fell apart under the assault of the pianist, usually at the worst moments, and it was not a happy spectacle—especially if the maker of that particular instrument was sitting in the audience that day.

Steinway's metal frame enhanced the longevity of the instrument by serving as a sturdy foundation for the entire action. Before Steinway first cast the bronze-alloy frame, piano actions were usually attached directly to the case, making it difficult to gain access to the parts and necessitating a custom fit for each instrument. Some actions were set in a wooden frame within the case, but the effects of weather often raised havoc with this design, causing the frame to swell and forcing the pieces out of alignment. Before the introduction of the cloverleaf-shaped frame, the word "inter-changeable" was not in the piano maker's lexicon. To complete this radical idea, Steinway mounted his metal frame on a wooden keybed, so that the whole business can slide in and out of the case with ease. A technician can simply remove a few blocks and slide the keyboard and action out for repair, or replace it altogether. When I was young, my brothers and I would drop pencils behind the keyboard lid when we

One complete action assembly. There are eighty-eight such actions in every piano.

Keybed

knew our uncle John Steinway was coming over, just so we could watch him disman-
tle our family's piano.

In addition to improving the serviceability of the piano, the tubular metal construction enhances the inherent advantages of both metal and wood. The seamless
brass tubes of the frame, onto which the wooden action assemblies are secured, are
filled with maple doweling. To ensure a tight fit between wood and metal, the doweling
is heated before insertion. As it cools, the wood expands, seating itself firmly. The
wooden action assemblies are then screwed through the tube into the doweling. This
allows for solid contact at the critical junction between the actions themselves and the
frame—the rigid metal ensures that the relative position of the individual action assemblies, all eighty-eight of them, remains true in any climate.

Steinway & Sons is the only American piano manufacturer to produce its
own piano actions. All the wooden parts are made in Long Island City, New York; the
felt and metal components are shipped in from outside suppliers but are finished in-
house. With fifty-eight parts in each action assembly, multiplied eighty-eight times
across the keyboard, the possibilities for trouble are manifold. Action work must be
meticulously done, and quality control is of paramount importance. By manufacturing
its own actions, Steinway can ensure a consistent level of workmanship.

The heart of an action assembly, called a whippen, can fit in your palm,
although some of the individual pieces are no bigger than the last joint on your little
finger. Fabricating these tiny wooden pieces is a fairly simple, but ingenious, process.
First, pieces of knot-free maple are glued together to form a solid block of a certain
size, depending on the dimensions of the finished piece. The block is then run over a
series of rotating blades, much like large routers, that shape the top, bottom, and sides.
The shaped block is next sliced like a loaf of bread to yield the individual parts. The
pieces are tumbled to remove burrs, sanded, and notched or drilled as necessary. Then
they are glued, pinned, or screwed into place within the whippen. Any surface that

rubs, butts into, pivots around, trips off of, or hinges on another is surfaced with a bushing material, usually leather or virgin wool felt, depending on the part's function. In some cases, when the parts need to move, the felt is impregnated with a fluid that leaves a slippery residue, which reduces friction.

The action assembly for each note is identical, but the hammer head—the part that hits the strings—is not. The hammer heads in the bass are larger, heavier, and pear-shaped in comparison with the ones in the treble, but all the hammer heads for a single piano are fashioned out of one continuous piece of virgin wool felt.

Almost every soft material has at one time been considered as a suitable covering for the piano hammers: parchment, various types of leather, metal, cloth, cork, gutta-percha, India rubber, sponge, and tinder—separately and sometimes in combination. Felt was settled upon as the most practical substance in the early 1800s, but many people still consider it to be less than ideal, since it eventually wears out and can be unruly to work with. In any event, it is the best we have. Many of the refinements in hammer design have been in adapting felt to its use.

The hammer is an extremely important link between the keyboard player and the sound, for it has to deliver the intended "message" to the strings without interference. In order to play both loud and soft in the bass as well as in the treble, the hammers must deliver both hard and soft blows to the strings with equal authority. To do this, the hammers must literally be both hard and soft at the same time. The elegant solution to this seeming paradox is to laminate two lengths of felt, of different densities, around a solid wooden core. Thick sheets of tapered felt arrive at the Steinway factory from an outside supplier. There they are preshaped on a sanding wheel, then glued around a birch center and molded under pressure. The softer felt is on the outside of the hammer, and the denser felt lies against the wood, which is very hard. After the molded baton, as it's called, is removed from the press, it is sanded again, then cut into eighty-eight pieces of like thickness. A tiny metal pin is driven through the felt on each hammer to ensure that the felt doesn't slip off the wooden core. Hammer shanks fashioned out of clear maple are fit into each piece, and the hammers are ready to go.

⚜

Assembly of the full action comes next. First, the whippens, all eighty-eight of them, are screwed into one of the dowels inside the metal action frame. Then the hammer shanks—which have each been pinned to a wooden piece called a flange that serves as a hinge—are fastened to the top of the frame. Finally, a series of "let-off" regulating screws are attached to the frame, one for each note. All the pieces are aligned and checked for ease of operation, and to make sure the hammer shanks are all parallel. If a hammer is out of alignment, the shank is heated with a low-temperature alcohol flame and gently twisted into place. Counting the regulating screws within the whippen itself, there are a total

A worker ensures that the hammer shanks are perfectly straight.

A section from
the tubular metal-
lic action frame.

of seven places where preliminary adjustments are made to each note. The entire compass is inspected several times to make sure all the individual actions work perfectly.

A model of a piano's action is a fascinating thing to behold. I used to play with one for hours on end when I was a child—pressing the key down again and again, trying to figure out how the thing worked and why it was necessary to have all those tiny levers, springs, pins, screws, knobs, plates, bushings, bearings, hinges, and flanges to do what seemed a simple task. The answer is that the piano's action has evolved over years of experimentation. Many of the recent innovations, however, have flopped. Modern materials, especially plastics, have not yet found a permanent place in a Steinway piano's action.

There is one part of the piano, though, where plastic has supplanted the older materials: the surface of the key itself. Over the years, piano keys have been covered with a variety of substances beyond the classic ebony and ivory. Different varieties of wood, elephant and walrus ivory, mother-of-pearl, tortoiseshell, cattle bone, and celluloid have all found their way onto piano keyboards at one time or another. Entrepreneurs from the Siberian tundra, in fact, recently offered Steinway "unlimited" amounts of fossilized mastodon tusk for this purpose—at a price.

While we may not be tickling the mammoth ivories any time soon, it is nearly certain that we will not be seeing fresh elephant ivory on the keyboard either. A 1975 treaty controlling the international trade of animal products derived from threatened species has put an end to the use of elephant ivory for any manufacturing purpose whatsoever. From the piano maker's perspective, though, ivory was always a problematic material. Piano manufacturers, by and large, loathed it. It was difficult and time consuming to match the ivory pieces for color and grain, and the material itself swells and shrinks according to the vagaries of weather, which accounted for a great amount of delamination. Ivory is also quite brittle. Most ivory keyboards you see today will at the very least be chipped along their leading edge, unless extreme care has been taken with the instrument. On the plus side, ivory is porous. Sweat can be readily absorbed, which can give the pianist's fingers a better grip. Ivorene, the synthetic material Steinway uses, has proved to be an acceptable substitute. Nonetheless, ivory has a unique feel, and although research continues, no material has been found that exactly duplicates all the properties of ivory.

Steinway & Sons, of its own volition, started putting plastic onto the keys in the 1950s, a decision that was greeted with little praise at the time. Within a few years, however, the decision became academic. Today the choice of material is out of the hands of the manufacturers; it is illegal even to import a piano with ivory keys into the United States unless it can be proved that the ivory is over one hundred years old. In some cases Steinway has provided a letter certifying that the ivory keys on a particular instrument are original, but even so it can be difficult to ship a piano with ivory keys internationally. Happily for the elephants, most piano lovers have adjusted to plastic keys, and the material itself has been improved to a point where some pianists actually prefer it. In the case of younger pianists, of course, this may be because plastic keys are all they have ever known.

The "ebony" keys, alas, are no longer ebony either; they, too, are plastic.

As for the distinctive black-and-white arrangement of the keyboard, this scheme, too, has seen its own vicissitudes. On many early instruments the colors are reversed, with blond wood on the sharps and flats. In the late nineteenth and early twentieth centuries there was a fad for "quarter-tone" music tuned to more than the standard twelve semitones, resulting in pianos constructed to suit. The extra keys were usually red and brown in color. For people who really can't make up their minds, there are pianos whose black keys sport a white stripe down the middle—aptly known as skunk's-tail keyboards. Regrettably, most of the instruments with this kind of key were made in the mid-1700s.

A complete keyboard-and-action assembly slides easily into the piano's case.

Steinway is the only piano manufacturer that bends the inner and outer rim in one piece.

THE RIM
AND THE CASE

RIM CLAMPS

The rim clamps were designed by C. F. Theodore Steinway.

OF ALL THE SIGHTS observed on a tour through the Steinway factory, the process of bending the rims is the most memorable. A piano's rim (the terms "rim" and "case" are more or less interchangeable) has to be many things at once: a strong support for the iron frame and the strings, a rock-solid base for the soundboard, a sturdy platform for the keyboard and action, and a beautifully finished piece of furniture. It is the shell of the piano, and at the same time its foundation.

This dual role is made possible by a two-part system that incorporates both an inner and an outer rim. If you cut a piano's case straight through from top to bottom, the cross section reveals different profiles on the inside and outside: the side facing out, the outer rim, is flat; but the side facing in, toward the strings, has a shelf in the middle. This "shelf" is actually the top of the piano's inner rim and is crucial to the Steinway's construction. The outer rim's job is to contain the vibration of the strings and soundboard and focus them inward, so as to maximize the volume of sound. The outer rim also contains the surface we see when we look at the instrument, so it must be able to accept a finish well. The inner rim is the foundation upon which the soundboard and frame lie, so it must be solid, capable of supporting a heavy weight.

Most piano manufacturers start with an inner rim and fit the soundboard to it, then shape an outer rim around that in a separate procedure. A great deal of structural integrity is lost with this method, resulting in a dissipation of vibration, and therefore sound. Steinway is unique in that it forms the inner and outer rims of the piano at the same time, in one integrated and continuous piece. The factory uses a method—and tools—devised by C. F. Theodore Steinway in the 1870s that has not fundamentally changed since.

A crew of six workers does nothing but bend rims. Their output will vary according to demand, but the pattern of their work is consistent. First, they select the materials to be used. The wood is maple, plain-sawed (because it bends more easily) and milled to a thickness of about $\frac{3}{16}$ inch. Matching the boards takes time because the knots must be removed, so the pieces come in different sizes and may have to be jointed to make a proper length. The grain of the wood is laid up to achieve maximum strength: the "inside" of one board (the side that grew closest to the center of the tree) is placed against the "outside" of the one facing it. Alternating the grain this way counterbalances each board's natural tendency to warp. All the surfaces that will be bonded together are scored so that the adhesive will gain a good hold on the wood.

The matched boards that will be laminated together into one rim are known as a book, and the number of laminations in a book varies with the size of the model. The rim of a (concert grand) model D, for example, is made up of eighteen layers of wood: nine to form the inner rim and nine wider ones for the outer rim. The rim of a model S (a "baby" grand, the smallest grand piano Steinway makes) contains twelve laminations. The thickness of the books ranges from $3\frac{1}{4}$ inches (model D), about as thick as a good college dictionary, to $2\frac{1}{8}$ inches for a baby grand. If the piano is to receive a natural rather than the black "ebonized" finish, the outermost laminate will be one continuous piece of the desired veneer.

After selecting and matching the wood, the crew hoists the book onto their

shoulders and walks the short distance to the basement room where the bending takes place. This large space contains eight massive piano-like forms, the molds for all the rims of all the Steinway pianos made in the United States. The first stop is the gluing bench. Since the rim for a concert grand has, at 22 feet, the longest book, the bench must be long enough to accommodate that length twice: before and after the boards pass through a device that applies the glue. This apparatus sits waist high, the height of the gluing bench, and looks like an old-fashioned washing machine—the kind with the rollers. Instead of squeezing moisture out of fabric, however, these rollers apply fresh glue to both sides of the boards as the workers pass them through. The foreman of the crew stands in the middle, at the rollers, with about half the men on one side feeding the boards in and half reassembling the book on the other. One worker hovers over the action, holding a bucket of glue and a paintbrush. His job is to hit any spots the rollers missed.

Many people assume that a piano's rim is one solid piece and are surprised to discover that it is made up of laminations. There are several reasons why this method is preferred. First, enough solid, knot-free maple boards of the proper dimensions

would be nearly impossible to find. Second, and more important for the instrument, a laminated rim is actually stronger. The multiple boards, the glue, and the balanced stresses of the grain add up to more than the sum of the parts in terms of strength. Additionally, a $\frac{1}{4}$-inch board is a lot easier to bend than one 4 inches thick, a fact appreciated by the crew every day. Later on, when they coerce the book around the mold, each laminate bends on its own, independent of the others. The wet glue acts as a lubricant, enabling the boards to slide against one another.

After the glue has been applied and the layers reassembled, the crew hoists the book once again and carries it over to the mold, where it will be bent into shape. The "wet" book is an ungainly thing, so the workers clasp a sheet of rough sandpaper between skin and wood to secure their grip. The inner side of the book is placed against the long, straight side of the appropriate mold and sandwiched between two thin, flexible sheets of copper. Each of these copper sheets has two electrical terminals, much like the terminals on the battery of a car, one at either end.

Once bending begins, it is an efficient operation. All the tools the crew will need have been set out within reach, and there is little talk. Each man knows his part

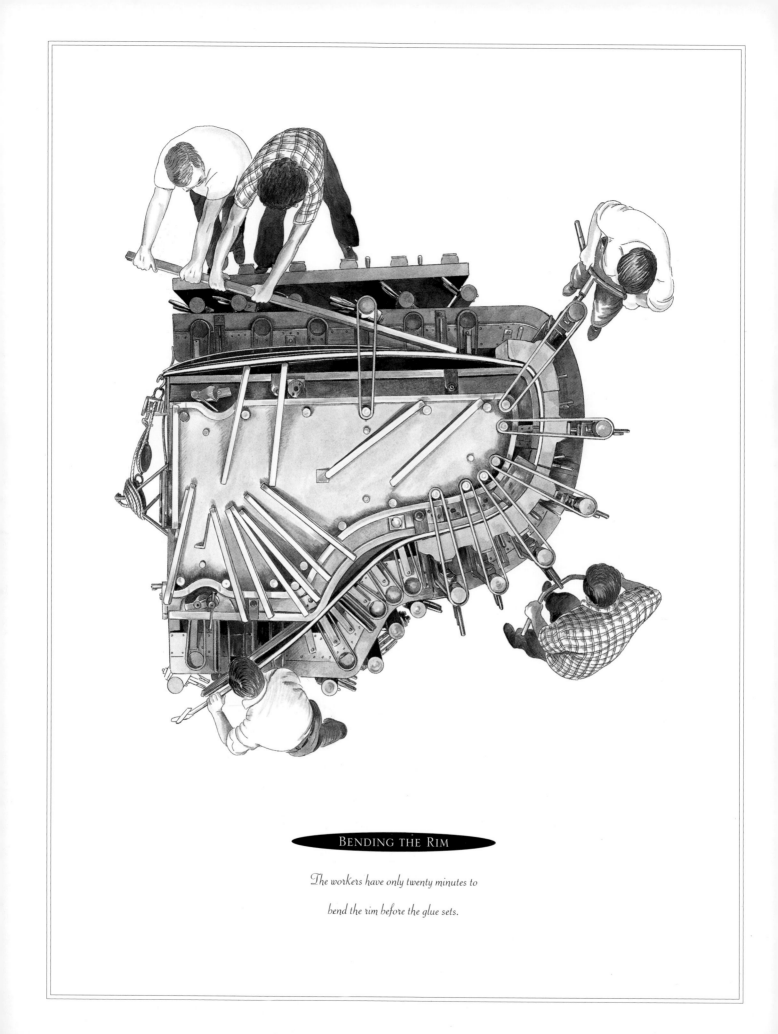

BENDING THE RIM

The workers have only twenty minutes to

bend the rim before the glue sets.

and goes about it with an efficiency that testifies both to his skill and to the team's mastery of the job at hand. They are about to shape 400 pounds of rock maple into curves as nature never intended—and they have about twenty minutes to accomplish the task before the glue sets. It's clearly a task that calls for solemn concentration.

They start attaching multipiece clamps, first along the straight side, beginning at the bass end of the keyboard. A heavy metal plate is placed along the outside of the book, then an upright piece that fits into slots along the bottom edge of the mold is set in position. The workers then put their shoulders into the recalcitrant wood, pressing it flush against the outer edge of the mold, and connect the top of the upright to the mold with a thick metal band, holding the plate fast against the wood. A large wing nut is screwed onto the outside of the upright piece to secure it all. This same pattern is repeated at various stations all along the perimeter of the rim.

Obviously, the first few feet are relatively easy—the curves are the tricky parts. The first two bends, at the end of the instrument farthest away from the keyboard, are the most difficult. The book has to take a 90-degree bend at that point, and then another one right away, almost folding back upon itself. Then the book has to be pushed into the familiar curve in the treble side of the piano, the niche where the singer stands framed by the piano in the classic recital pose. Lastly, the rim is bent nearly 90 degrees once more, making one final curve back toward the treble end of the keyboard and ending exactly parallel to where it started. No power tools help persuade the wood in this operation, just leverage and brute force.

As most of the crew grunt and shove the book into its new shape, one man follows along the main part of the crew with a mallet and a block of wood, pounding down on the top edge of the laminates to make sure they are properly aligned. As the men move toward the treble end of the piano, nearly completing the circuit, another worker begins to secure the wing nuts on the clamps, starting at the bass end, using a metal T-bar and then tightening them with a hydraulic wrench. Some excess glue will

The bent rims season in a climate-controlled environment.

usually get squeezed out from between the laminates by the compression, and the workers wipe it away with a damp rag.

Finally, the crew attaches the electrodes on the copper plates to a transformer, which sends a continuous low voltage through the mass, a "high-frequency" glue-curing system patented by Steinway & Sons in 1947. This technique was developed during World War II, when the factory was making parts for wooden gliders as well as small "GI" pianos for field use by U.S. armed forces. It ensures both maximum catalytic action in the urea resin glue and the strongest possible bond in the rim.

At the end of the job the crew unceremoniously walks away, to begin the process once more.

The rim is left on its mold for twenty-four hours, then it is removed and chalked with the date, size, and veneer type, if appropriate. You might think that the wood's "memory" would open up the rim, but instead the sides tend to pinch inward, so a brace is placed between the open ends. After a few days the rim is moved upstairs and placed in a temperature- and humidity-controlled chamber to rest for at least ten weeks. This gives the rim a chance to settle into its new configuration, and the moisture content to return to the optimal, about 6 percent. By then the wood has accepted its new shape, which it will hold forevermore.

The next step is called fraizing. This entails trimming the rim to its final dimensions, shaping the rough edges, and sanding all the surfaces to give a better grip for whatever finish the piano will receive. Fraizing is done on a large stationary routing table; the entire piano rim moves, and the cutting blade stays put. It is also at this stage where the wrestplank, or pin block, is attached to the rim with maple dowels.

After fraizing, the rim is moved to the "case-making" department, where internal braces and a keybed are installed. The bracing inside the case is especially important, and the arrangement of spruce blocks and "treble bells," unseen except from below the instrument, differs from model to model. The cast-iron bells attach to the inside of the rim at the piano's treble bend and serve as a fixed mounting point for the iron frame. The spruce braces are all affixed with maple doweling, which affords a permanent rim posture.

Aside from the bent rim, the case of the piano is made up of four other ele-

Intricate wood carving is done by hand.

ments: the keylid, top, music desk, and legs. Piano people refer to the hinged panel that covers the strings as the "top"; they reserve the word "lid" for the curved cover that pivots up to expose the keys and has the maker's mark centered on it. The top is a large, flat panel that can be propped up on an angled rod (the topstick) to project the maximum amount of sound toward the audience. The topstick has a shorter rod mounted within it, which can be used to prop the top open partway, for a lesser pro-jection of sound. Since the top can be easily attached only to the straight (bass) side of the case, hinging upward like a clamshell, nearly every pianist positions the instrument

CASE WORKER

The Steinway factory lies close to

midtown Manhattan.

with the treble side facing the audience when they perform. And it is why tickets for a piano recital often sell out on the left side of the auditorium first: most of us prefer to see the artist's hands when he plays. The music desk, which holds the pages in front of the player, can slide back and forth and can be easily removed altogether. The legs are fashioned in a separate department of the factory; they, too, can be readily removed in order to facilitate moving the piano.

Music desk,

c. 1885.

No discussion of the rim and the case would be complete without mentioning two other aspects of the subject: wood carving and "art-case" pianos.

Carved wood is an essential part of several models of the Steinway piano being made today and of many of the ones from yesteryear. The fancy embellishments on the "Chippendale" and "Louis XV" models are created in-house from blocks of solid mahogany or black walnut, depending on the case wood of the finished piano. It is and always has been difficult to find craftspeople skilled in this trade. Only a handful of people, many with the same last name, have been employed at it during the firm's history. The department is presently made up of two full-time wood carvers and two apprentices. These few people are responsible for all the decorative carving on all the American Steinways.

The art-case pianos, usually one-of-a-kind instruments, are a long tradition at Steinway & Sons. Over the years the firm has created a number of specially designed and crafted pianos for a select circle of clients. Unique pianos have been crafted to suit both fashion and fancy. Some of these instruments have remained with the original owners, while many of them have been resold, sometimes at considerable profit. In 1980, for example, an ornate concert grand crafted in 1883 for the president of New York's Metropolitan Museum of Art and decorated by the noted Victorian artist Sir Lawrence Alma-Tadema was sold at auction for the sum of $360,000. At the time this was the highest price ever paid for a piano. Until recently the instrument was on display in the Museum of Fine Arts, Boston. New art-case pianos can still be had for a price, and there is a burgeoning market for the old ones. Often an art-case piano created by, or credited to, a famous furniture maker or designer can be purchased for a fraction of the price of a comparable piece made by the same person.

The East Room of the White House is home to what is probably the best-known art-case Steinway piano, serial number 300,000, which was presented as a gift from the Steinway family to the people of the United States in 1938. This 10½ foot concert grand piano has an extended mahogany case designed by the noted New York architect Eric Gugler. The front side of the case is decorated with five gold leaf tableaux by Dunbar Beck representing American music: "The Virgina Reel," "The Chant of the American Indian," "The Song of the Cowboy," "The Barn Dance," and "The Song of the Black Slave." The ornately carved golden eagles that support the case are the work of Albert Stewart. This instrument has undergone a complete refurbishing at the Steinway factory and was returned to its home in Washington, D.C., in 1992. It is used for concerts and recitals on a regular basis. This is the second piano that Steinway & Sons has presented to the nation—serial number 100,000, an ornate gilded grand, was delivered to President Theodore Roosevelt in 1903. This instrument is currently in the collection of the National Museum of American History at the Smithsonian Institution in Washington, D.C.

It can be said that a piano is the perfect example of form following function. Despite this arguable fact, many noted artists, architects, furniture makers, and industrial designers have taken a crack at redesigning the instrument over the years, with varying degrees of success. At one time or another Jules Bouy, Wendell Castle,

George Denninger, George Shastey, Walter Dorwin Teague, Tenboom, Joseph Burr Tiffany, the Herter Brothers, the Hunt Brothers, and Pottier and Stymus have all created instruments bearing the Steinway name. In some instances the designers were presented with an unfinished instrument for elaboration, and in other instances they worked with the craftsmen at Steinway & Sons to create a piano case from scratch. The art-case department has not limited their activities strictly to collaborations with these artisans, however. Often they have worked directly with the customers themselves. Unique pianos have been crafted to fit everything from outsized egos to living room curtains, and turn up everywhere from a yacht's interior to the concert stage.

THE HARP
AND THE STRINGS

The cast-iron cupola frame

lies at the heart of every

Steinway piano.

IN THE LONG HISTORY of the instrument called piano, probably the single greatest technological leap was the introduction of the one-piece iron frame, or harp, to hold the strings. This honor belongs to an American, Alpheus Babcock, who patented his invention in Boston in 1825. There had been experiments with the use of metal inside the piano's case before that time, but Babcock put the design of the instrument on a path from which it has never strayed. There were many drawbacks to Babcock's invention, however—buzzing notes, a thin treble, and loose tuning pins being the primary ones—and the innovation was considered a novelty until it was refined and later perfected by Steinway & Sons.

The biggest problem facing piano manufacturers at the turn of the nineteenth century was the inescapable fact that greater string tension, which was needed to increase volume, produced a host of complications. A wooden box, no matter how carefully constructed, simply cannot undergo the constant tug of metal strings without yielding. Two main problems arise: the box itself is pulled out of shape, an effect called cheek warp, and the instrument quickly goes out of tune. Climatic changes also cause difficulties with wood.

Babcock's original frame was designed for a square piano, but it was in the grand pianos where the iron frame really came into its own. The grands are the ultimate expression of the piano maker's craft, and they always attracted the most attention at the great industrial fairs of the mid-1800s. It was at these meetings where the worlds of art, science, and commerce met, and in this arena reputations, and successful businesses, were created and destroyed.

The central feature of the Steinway system, the overstrung one-piece iron frame that brought the company so much glory in 1867, was in use by Steinway & Sons as early as 1860. The company approached this new technology in stages; each innovation they made (the agraffe, the overstringing, and so on) was a step toward overcoming the limitations of Babcock's basic idea. The improvements they sought are easy to summarize: longer, heavier strings under greater tension for volume; the opportunity to move the bridge closer to the center of the soundboard for tone; and the advantages of metal for durability. Part of the solution, the company found, was to place the tuning peg in a block of wood butting up directly against the iron frame, while the other end of the string attached directly to the frame itself at the hitch pin. This way the advantages of setting the tuning pin in wood were combined with the strength of the metal frame to absorb tension. Great amounts of tension. Some 70,000 pounds of tension to be precise. Once string tensions like that were achieved, there was no turning back from this design.

Sand casting is a process that has not fundamentally changed since the days of the ancient Egyptians. To be sure, there have been countless improvements in materials and technique since that time, but the basic technique looks marvelously archaic to our eyes today. It is a two-step process that involves a different set of workers for the casting of the "gray iron," or cast-iron frame itself, and the finishing of that crucial piece into the golden harp that you see under the piano's top. At every step the frame is inspected for quality and appearance, and indeed many harps are rejected along the way for any number of reasons. This can happen at any moment from the time the molten metal is poured, up until the finished harp is about to be installed inside the piano's rim.

It has been several decades since the company last poured iron in Long Island City; this is one of the few parts of the piano (the keys, strings, and felt are others) for which the factory depends on outside suppliers. The master patterns, however, are exclusively Steinway's.

MOLD-MAKING

A new mold is created for each frame. It is destroyed

when the harp is pulled from the sand.

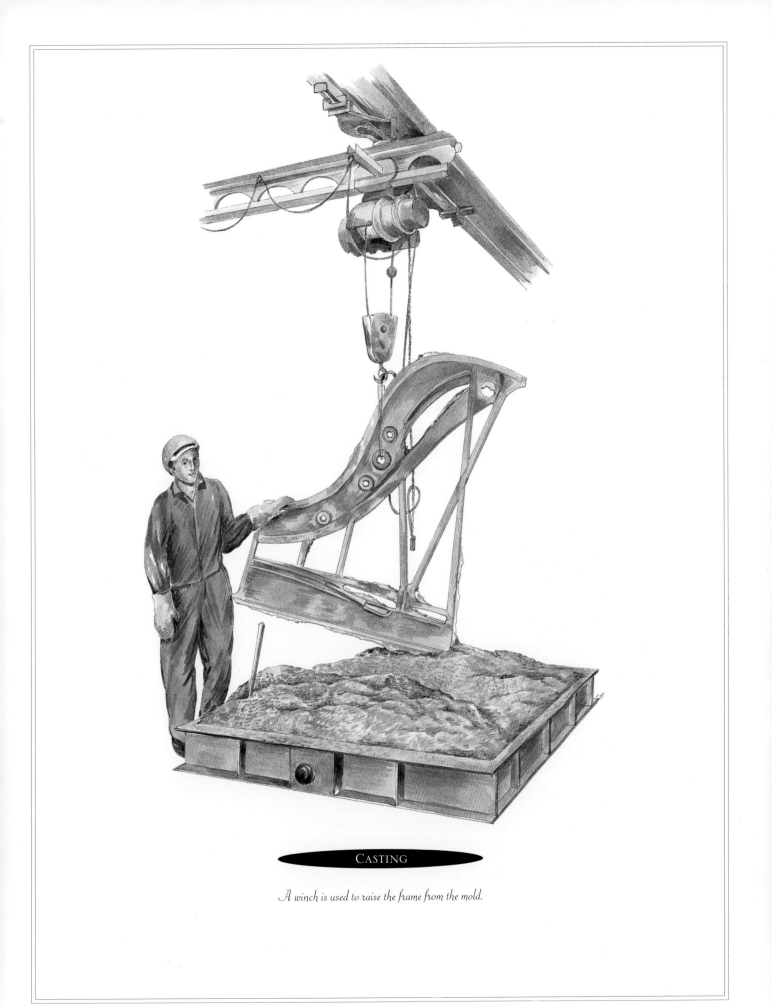

CASTING

A winch is used to raise the frame from the mold.

A crew of two is responsible for the casting. The first thing the workers do is fabricate a mold. At the foundry this is known as a floor-mold process, since because the molds are necessarily large, the work is done on the factory's floor. There are two halves to every mold—the top is known as the cope, and the bottom half is called the drag—and for every piano's frame a new mold is taken off of the master pattern that looks to all appearances like a wooden platform. There are two bottom, for each size instrument first step in the mold-making face of each master with a fine prevent the sand from sticking withdrawn. Then a rectangular  piano frame screwed onto a of these masters, top and the company makes. The process is to spray the sur- mist of lubricating fluid to to the pattern when the mold is frame crisscrossed with flat metal bars, called a flask, is placed on top of the pattern. The bars create a series of little box-shaped spaces that help to hold the sand in place.

The sand itself is jet black and very fine and comes from the beaches of the Great Lakes. This, along with the availability of iron ore, is why the midwestern states of Ohio and Indiana are the centers of gray-iron production in the United States. It is hard to tell what color the sand was originally, as it has been mixed both with powdered clay, which helps it retain shape, and with ground coal, which helps fix the surface of the metal when the iron is poured.

In the foundry, this black sand is omnipresent—cascading into hoppers from bins set in the ceiling, underfoot everywhere, and heavy in the air with a burnt charcoal fragrance that stays with you for days. After an hour, the smell of it, and its blackness, penetrate your clothes as well as your nasal passages. An iron foundry is not a place to wear tennis whites, nor is it a place where one's respiratory health is served. It is a site of heavy manufacture, one that vividly recalls the sooty darkness of the Industrial Age.

The sand is first sifted through the open spaces in the flask directly onto the master, completely obliterating the form beneath in just a few minutes. The level of sifted sand is then brought up to where the plates on the flask just begin, and the workers add more sand by the shovelful until the little boxes within the flask are heaped with the stuff. Then the sand is tamped down with a hand-held pneumatic hammer so that every crevice of the master is filled (including the dinner-plate-sized Steinway & Sons emblem at the treble end) and the compressed sand takes on some slight structural integrity of its own. A bigger load of sand is dumped on top, and the material is spread out and tamped down again and again until the flask is full—a kind of industrial sandbox with a treasure inside.

These steps are then repeated with both sides of the mold. At the hitch-pin end of the cope (the top half), the workers punch a wrist-sized hole, where the molten iron will be poured in. They also make two smaller vent holes on its other end, where air can escape as the liquid metal fills the cavity, although since sand is porous, some of the air and steam is able to pass right through it. The cope and the drag are then lifted off their respective masters and placed on top of one another, with two large pins between them to ensure a proper fit. C-clamps are then secured around the perimeter of the two parts, making a single unit of the two, and the workers move off to collect a batch of molten iron.

The metal is a cocktail of pig iron, scrap steel, and what is known as remelt, which is recycled bits from the foundry. To ensure proper crystalline structure as it cools, the mixture is laced with silicon, carbon, and manganese before it enters the mold. This gray iron is cooked up each night in round, room-sized furnaces—nights, because that's when the electric power rates are low. During the day, the iron is "simply" held at a temperature of about 3,000 degrees Fahrenheit. The three furnaces are shut down only a few times a year, to undergo relining. These lidded furnaces look like immense smiling demons, the glowing metal inside them barely visible except for a curved line from under the lid shining out brightly within the darkness of the foundry.

It is as easy to say that the workers draw off a ladleful of iron as it is to say that they place the cope on top of the drag, but keep in mind that these are industrial practices, so the scale makes the process a bit different than ladling out the gravy from a kitchen roasting pan. The upper reaches of the foundry are a maze of track, with winches and cables to suspend and transport the molten iron. Protective gear and a face mask are in order, and during my visit a worker casually mentioned that it might be a good idea if I didn't turn my back as the molten metal was poured into the mold. He was right—molten gobbets of liquid metal and sparks fly in all directions, and they can burn severely if they touch your body or your clothing.

After the metal is taken from the furnace, the workers have about ten minutes to pour the mold, and not a movement is wasted during that time. When the thin stream of crimson iron falls from the bucket and fills out the sand, the entire mold begins to smolder as the coal and the clay are vaporized in an instant. The workers pour two frames at a time, and once the metal is in place, it is usually a good time for a lunch break. Although it takes only a few minutes for the liquid to solid-ify, it stays hot for hours.

When the clamps and the pins are removed and the cope is lifted away from the drag, there is another emanation of steamy vapor as more hot sand is exposed to the air. The cope is cleaned out and put aside, and the workers bring the winch back to hover over the drag portion of the mold. The hook is lowered to the sandy surface, the worker roots around and attaches it to the iron shape within and then gives a signal, and a completed casting slowly rises up from the blackness like hope from the ashes of despair. As it hangs in the stygian darkness, the crew casually knocks away extraneous pieces of metal that may have formed in spaces between the cope and drag. The process works. It worked for the ancient Egyptians, and it works today.

Finishing a harp is a slower affair, involving more people, more tools, and more steps. The gray-iron frame is first given a thorough inspection to make sure that all the elevations where the strings will go are formed correctly. A computer-guided tool is then used to drill all the necessary holes: for the bolts that will fasten the harp to the inner rim of the piano, the tuning pins, the agraffes, and the hitch pins. Some of these holes must be drilled at precise angles, which are checked later on. The computer is a help in this, one of the few examples where technology introduced in the last few years has really improved the process.

Every surface of the frame is then ground by hand to remove burrs and imperfections and to prepare it to receive its finish. At this stage the V-bar, or capo d'astro (which

Heavier strings can be held under greater tension, producing a bigger sound.

replaces the agraffe in the treble notes), on the frame's underside is given a patented treatment that hardens it considerably. The entire frame is then baked at a temperature of 500 degrees Fahrenheit for forty-five minutes, to release gases within the iron. Once it has cooled to 300 degrees, the frame is gently sprayed with an epoxy powder that melts when it comes into contact with the hot metal, and the frame takes on a shiny black look. Then the frame is baked again, to cure the epoxy. Next the epoxy is removed, by hand, from surfaces where it is not needed (such as where the iron meets the wood of the wrestplank) and the entire frame is hand-sanded to roughen the slick coating's surface. At this stage, the frame has a dull black appearance. Then the golden color is applied— finely powdered brass suspended in a lacquer base. More sanding, polishing, and at least three more coats of lacquer, and the lustrous yellow patina familiar to all piano lovers is finally achieved. The hitch pins and agraffes are installed, and the final step in the process is the careful lettering, by hand, of the raised letters STEINWAY, the model code, and the familiar lyre emblem.

A piano's strings, naturally, must be extremely strong to be held under such huge tension as the iron frame is capable of withstanding. In this area, as in nearly every other facet of the modern piano, there has been a great deal of experimentation. It is hard to determine what materials the earliest instruments were strung with, as often the strings on the historical pianos have been replaced, but generally speaking the piano string has evolved from soft iron to hard steel, with or without a wrapping of brass or copper. Today's Steinway pianos are strung with up to twelve different sizes of wire, depending on the model. All of the strings are fabricated from high-tensile steel, and the wrapped strings are covered with pure copper.

During World War II, copper and, to a certain extent, steel were considered strategic materials and therefore were practically unavailable for pianos. This cut back production at the factory considerably, but the workers were not completely idle. A specially designed "Victory" model upright piano, less formally known as the "Olive

Drab Government Issue" (ODGI) field piano, was created for the U.S. Armed Forces. This instrument was packed in its own traveling case, which also contained a set of tuning tools, some spare parts, a manual, and some sheet music. Its strings were made from steel wrapped with iron. The company produced almost 3,000 of these durable pianos.

My uncle Henry Steinway married during the war years, and his father, who was president of the company at the time, presented the couple with a grand piano as a wedding gift. The instrument, which sits in my uncle's living room today, has soft iron strings.

A single "belly man" is responsible for the fit of the soundboard and harp.

ASSEMBLY

HAVING SEEN HOW the individual components of a piano are fabricated, we now see how they come together. The rim has been bent and fashioned into what can now be called a case, the soundboard and bridge have been assembled, and the harp has been cast and finished. If the instrument is to reach its full potential for sound, these three major elements need to fit together perfectly. This happens in a section of the factory appropriately known as the "belly" department, since these are the "guts" of the instrument. It is the first of many steps in the custom fitting of a piano and the beginning of the process that creates an instrument of a singular nature out of an agglomeration of pieces.

While there have been some quantum leaps in piano design, the small gains are truly what have given the piano its full power. Likewise, "God is in the details" when it comes to piano construction. The pieces have to be made well, but they must fit together perfectly, seamlessly, so that the simple act of placing a finger upon the key will produce a sound that can fill Carnegie Hall. Assembly of the piano is therefore a crucial step. Fitting the soundboard to the case alone is a job that in the early days the Steinway men saved exclusively for themselves. It is that important.

Imagine that you have just received a model airplane as a present. On the top of the box is a picture of a beautiful aerodynamic shape soaring through space, but inside is a mass of balsa wood, a few sheets of tissue paper, a plastic propeller, some wire bits, a rubber band, and a large instruction sheet. Patiently, you assemble the constituent elements—the fuselage, wings, and tail. The job seems easier when broken down, but if everything doesn't fit right, the model airplane will never fly. Now imagine that instead of being able to lay out the project on the dining room table, you are on the factory floor and you can't even lift some of the parts because they weigh more than you do. You may now have an idea of the enormity of the task that lies ahead.

At Steinway & Sons, pianos are not created on an assembly line. "The factory" is not a single structure but a collection of buildings, some dating to the 1800s, where various tasks have been performed at different times during the company's history. The physical plant has been altered to accommodate the construction of the instruments, not vice versa, and modifications have always been made in the flow of pieces from one department to another. Through it all, the belly department has been the place where the major components are fit together, and one worker per piano has always been responsible for this crucial phase of construction. Many of the tools are still the same as in the old days—hand tools mostly, such as planes, scrapers, hammers, chisels, drills, fasteners, string, lead weights, pencils, and sandpaper. This is not because of stubbornness on the company's part. These tools are simply more suited to the task of custom work. Two things have changed, however. The drill is now an electric power drill instead of a brace-and-bit, and a small motor powers the machinery that raises and lowers the harp.

The piano's components are not pieces that have been stamped out by a machine and assembled by robots. The Steinway piano is assembled by hand. It has to be, because every piece of wood is unique. Every board or block will be slightly different from another, even from one that was cut from the same log. So every component will differ slightly from another and must be treated individually. The fitting must be done by hand. Machinery cannot replace trained workers; it can only assist them. In the Steinway & Sons factory, high technology is used only for the simplest jobs. Even the fanciest, well-programmed, computerized, laser-guided, diamond-tipped cutting machine would have to be instructed by a human as to just how much wood to remove to make a perfect fit between two pieces with as many curvilinear surfaces as a soundboard and a piano rim. Some piano makers use machinery for such an important job, but not here; the pianos are built to a standard, not a price. High technology is used to complement the craftsman, not the other way around.

The highly skilled worker, known as a belly man, usually works on two instruments at the same time, since he can begin to assemble one piano while the glue on another one dries. A single workbench, with tools carefully arranged for efficiency, stands between the two pianos. Above each of them hangs a finished iron frame, suspended from pulleys attached to the ceiling. In a rack close by lie two soundboards, their bridges glued in place. The harp has been previously ground to fit the inner rim of the case, and the soundboard has been fashioned with extra material around its outside edge. The latter is done on purpose, for the fitting of the soundboard to the inner rim is the key task.

The belly man's job is not only to fit the components tightly to the case but also to determine the final height of the bridge. This second task is a critical one, for it dictates the amount of pressure the strings will exert downward onto the soundboard. Too much downward pressure will force the soundboard out of shape and

The Action

muffle the sound. Too little pressure, and the sound will be too thin. The process of adjusting the height of the bridge is called "taking the bearing," that is, assessing the pressure of the strings on the soundboard. Proper bearing ensures that each string will pass from the agraffe on the keyboard end, or the capo d'astro bar in the case of the upper treble notes; rise a precise amount up and over the bridge; then descend at the proper angle to the hitch pin at the far end. Adjusting the bearing involves lowering the top of the bridge to the appropriate level, but this is not done until a few other tasks have been performed.

First, the soundboard must be fit to the case, and its front height must be fixed.

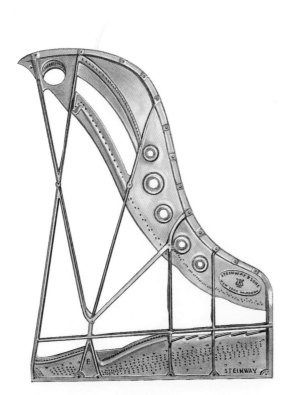

The Harp

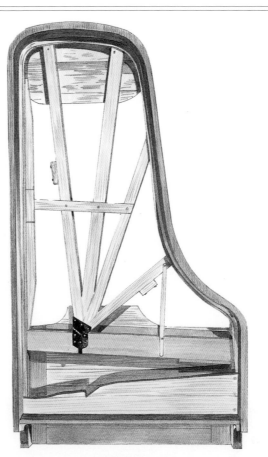

The Case

The Keyboard

Leg

Pedal Lyre

Leg

Although the rims are all bent on the same molds, each one varies slightly—wood works like that—and so a soundboard must be custom-fit in order for full contact to be made all the way around. A modified routing tool, similar to the one used in fraizing, is employed for this primary task. The tool is placed within the piano's rim and coupled to the soundboard that is going inside it. The soundboard is suspended above, held by suction so that nothing intrudes upon its edges, and the tool moves, tracing the actual contour of the inside of the rim at the same time as it shapes the outer edge of the soundboard. A perfect, gap-free fit is the result. The front edge of the soundboard, facing the keys, sits on a rail made of birch and topped with spruce that the belly man installs when he knows the back end of it fits properly.

The edge of the wrestplank that faces the harp also has to fit perfectly, because otherwise the tension of the strings pulling the wood toward the metal would wreak havoc. This fitting is done by an exacting hand process. The leading flange on the harp, the part that butts up against the wood, is coated with a thick graphite paste. The harp is lowered into the case, and the paste leaves a smudge on the wooden wrestplank that shows where contact has been made. The harp is removed, and the high spot is planed until the smudge disappears. The harp is then lowered into the case once again and raised again for inspection. The process is repeated until the graphite paste leaves a continuous band along the entire edge of the wrestplank, which demonstrates that full contact is being made.

After the rim, soundboard, and harp have been carefully modified to fit one another perfectly, but before the pieces are permanently fastened together, the exacting work of taking the bearing and notching the bridge is done. The soundboard and harp are laid inside the case just as they will rest inside the finished piano and are temporarily clamped in place. The worker then takes out a simple kit consisting of a couple of lengths of thick string and some flat pieces of metal about the size of a postage stamp, each identified as to its thickness. These, plus a pot of graphite paste, a handful of steel pins, a drill, a handsaw, a hammer, a file, and a chisel, are all that the worker needs for this next procedure.

To take the bearing, the worker stretches a piece of string through the agraffe, over the bridge, and back to the rear of the plate as though it were an actual piano string. Just in front of the point where the far end of the string meets the hitch pin, he places a "bearing block" (one of the stamp-sized metal pieces) which slightly raises the level. Since the height of both the front end of the string (at the agraffe) and the rear end (at the hitch pin) are predetermined by the shape of the metal harp, the bridge is the only spot in the assembly where a height adjustment can easily be made. The bearing block is the same thickness as the desired rise and fall of the string at that point of the keyboard. If the bridge is the correct height, the string should lie flat from end to end, so that the string achieves the desired arc after the bearing block is removed. Because the bridge was originally constructed with extra height, the string will, at this time, have a noticeable peak at the point where it passes over the cap. The worker carefully saws a shallow gash in the top of the bridge directly beneath the string, stepping back to look, wiggling the string, and deepening the cut as needed until the string lies perfectly flat. Once it does, the worker knows that the bottom of the gash is the proper height for the finished bridge. He then colors the bottom of the trench with a thick pencil.

This maneuver is repeated at fourteen points along the compass.

The harp is then removed from the case, and the soundboard is lifted out and set down on the workbench. The belly man is now looking at the flat surface of a bridge with fourteen gashes along its length that indicate the correct height. From here it is a matter of carefully planing the entire surface of the bridge until the pencil marks nearly disappear.

Then the bridge pins (486 of them in a concert grand) need to be installed, and the top of the bridge must be notched. This step creates the bridge's distinctive zigzag pattern. The pattern is certainly decorative, but the notching is done for an important reason: the string must contact the bridge at the exact same point where it contacts the bridge pin. If it doesn't, the vibration of the string will dissipate somewhat, and the note will sound "confused." The bridge pins delineate the desired contact surface between string and bridge; the rest of the surface wood is extraneous and should be removed.

First, holes for the pins are drilled in the maple. Next, the entire surface of the bridge is coated with graphite paste and hand-rubbed to burnish the material into the wood's surface. The steel-plated copper pins are then inserted into the holes and filed

Taking the
bearing.

down to their proper stubby height. Once this is done, the belly man, using a sharp wide-faced chisel, makes a series of right-angle cuts just fore and aft of the pins. The entire job takes most of a day.

When it is done, a team of helpers arrives to glue the soundboard into place on top of the inner rim. Large clamps are applied all around the perimeter of the piano to keep the soundboard in place. After a few hours, once the glue has set, the clamps are removed, dowels are installed that keep the metal harp from contacting the soundboard directly, and the harp is lowered into the case once again for a final check for fit. The

CRAFTSMAN

The distinctive zigzag pattern on the bridge

is chiseled by hand.

belly man makes a last inspection to see that the bearing is correct along the entire length of the bridge, and his job is complete.

The piano then moves along to other workers, who apply finish to the soundboard and bolt the harp in place. Two coats of sealer are used to fill the pores of the soundboard spruce, and a final coat of varnish is applied. The correct amount of varnish is poured on and allowed to flow freely over the entire surface of the wood without brushing—this accounts for the mirrorlike finish you see on the soundboard. The iron frame is then bolted through the soundboard in such a way that no contact is made between the metal and the soundboard itself. This acoustic dowel construction, which Steinway first patented in 1898, ensures that the soundboard can vibrate freely, independent of the massive weight of metal that rests just above it.

The piano now receives its strings. On a concert grand and the model B (the next smaller size), the pattern goes like this: The lowest eight notes get one string apiece, wrapped around the tuning peg at the near end and tied off around the hitch pin at the other.

The soundboard and chiseled bridge of Steinway Model B.

The next five notes get two strings apiece. These, too, are tied off individually. The rest of the compass receives three strings for each note. Of these, the strings for the seven lowest notes are tied off.

For the rest of the notes, the strings are looped around the hitch pin at the far end. It is easy to see when you look under the top: the bass notes that lie over the treble strings (all the overstrung notes) tie off around the hitch pin; the remaining strings all loop around the hitch pins. The tremendous amount of tension under which these strings are held makes it possible for a single piece of wire, looped around a hitch pin, to be tuned to two different frequencies.

Bringing a piano in tune to pitch, however, is a different story. The stringer does what he can to approximate the correct pitch, but the strings need to break in, so they will require nearly constant tuning in the days ahead as they adjust to their new state. In fact, the entire instrument needs a period of time to "cure."

After the piano leaves the belly department, it can no longer be considered a collection of parts; it is well on its way to becoming a musical instrument. One could easily get a keyboard and action from the action department, slide it in place, and play away—but it wouldn't sound like a Steinway. Likewise, attaching a set of pedals, three legs, and a top would not make it look like one either. It takes more than that.

Acoustic dowels keep the heavy iron plate from interfering with the vibrations of the soundboard.

Franz Mohr, master technician, worked with many famous Steinway artists for more than 30 years.

VOICING

IN 1774, the French philosopher and social wit Voltaire dismissed the pianoforte as an inferior instrument and compared its sound to that produced by "a tinker's kettle." No doubt Voltaire drew his conclusions after listening to the best instruments of his day, but his remark could equally apply to a brand-new piano that has not been through the transformative process called voicing.

Of all the facets of piano construction, voicing is the most often misunderstood and the least immediately apparent to the untrained hand and ear—but it is critical. During this final period, the piano undergoes a metamorphosis from a machine capable of producing sound into an instrument capable of making music. This is the stage where magic, or at least wizardry, can happen; where a prosaic model can suddenly become the favorite of a Horowitz or a Rubinstein. The process brings out a particular instrument's unique nature—the qualities of touch, feel, and sound that can make one piano totally different from another, even though they may have been made from the same materials, at the same time, and by the same hands. This phenomenon is no secret to a performing artist who regularly plays on different instruments, but it is often surprising to the average customer. People interested in a Steinway & Sons grand piano are encouraged to try out several different instruments before they choose one for themselves.

Voicing is the preparation the piano receives after it has been built but before it is shipped from the factory. The word "voicing" is used here in its most general sense, because the full process involves much more than simply fiddling with the hammers to regulate the tone and "give voice" to the instrument. Various workers will repeatedly adjust, tune, tone, regulate, and balance parts of the instrument to ensure the evenness of sound and regularity of touch across the entire keyboard.

Since a piano is made basically of wood, a substance that was once alive, each instrument has individual characteristics that reveal themselves over time, much as a baby evinces a personality at birth that may change as the child grows older. A large part of the voicing process involves eliciting a piano's peculiarities, discovering what the "personality" of the particular instrument may be, and dealing with it early on. Because an adjustment in one area of the piano typically causes a reaction in another, and because the strings, bridge and soundboard, action, and any other parts that are held under pressure have a certain "settling in" period at the beginning, these tasks are performed over and over again until the essential nature of an individual instrument is uncovered and either nurtured or moderated.

The action, for example, needs to be worked in. Any parts that malfunction or break in the course of normal use must be replaced. The action must also be regulated so that the treble end gives slightly more acceleration to the hammer for the same touch than the bass, because the treble strings don't excite as easily. The keyboard must fit like skin to the case, and it must be able to slide easily and noiselessly ⅛ inch to the right, toward the treble end, when the left (soft) pedal is depressed. The hammers must be given their final shaping, and their firmness must be adjusted. The strings need to be tuned again and again, until they hold fast to pitch. If one of them doesn't excite easily, doesn't vibrate fully, buzzes, or doesn't satisfy for whatever reason, it too must be replaced. The keys have to be individually balanced for touch and adjusted for height. The keyboard as a whole must be given a slight crown, rising in the center, because the middle keys are used the most and over time will sink slightly from use.

To accelerate this breaking in, Steinway uses a robotic device called either a sounder, a banger, or a pounder, depending on whom you ask. This mechanical apparatus fits over the keyboard much like an antique pianola and pounds every note on the piano about 8,000 times in the space of forty-five minutes. Two of these machines are on hand, pounding away at every keyboard of every piano Steinway ships. They are isolated in a relatively untraveled part of the factory in somewhat soundproof booths.

WEIGHTING KEYS

Lead weights are installed in the keys for balance.

Even so, you can imagine the cacophony. This is an important step, though, because the action needs to be worked, as does any piece of machinery built to give dependable service for a long period of time. Immediately after the intense pounding session, the action is inspected and any faulty parts are replaced.

The keys, which arrive from a supplier in Germany in matched sets, are then individually weighted with lead to give an even touch across the compass. About 50 grams of pressure is the standard for depression, 19 for the rise. This means that it takes the keyboard player less than 2 ounces of downward pressure to sound a note (this would be an ultraquiet note!), but about one-third of that force is needed to return the hammer to its "ready" position and for the key to rise. The upper end of the register is where most of the trills occur, so these forces are calibrated accordingly in the treble end. A small "repetition" spring within the action is also adjustable.

Some pianists prefer a different feel, however, and their preferences can usually be accommodated. Vladimir Horowitz, for example, had a fondness for an especially responsive, light touch (Horowitz was consulted regularly when the company was developing its patented "accelerated action" in the 1930s), whereas Arthur Rubinstein wished a more resistant touch from the keys and a darker, more basso sound. Glenn Gould also liked a harder touch, more akin to the harpsichord, for certain pieces of music, especially his unique Bach interpretations. For other composers, such as Richard Strauss, Gould preferred what he called a "shallow" touch. These instruments were regulated to such a hair-trigger degree that some of his recordings contain what Gould himself referred to as "hiccups," which accidentally sounded a single note twice for one touch of the key. Gould was charmed by the effect, much to the chagrin of his record producers and, it is assumed, the composer, were he around to hear it.

Other pianists have desired an extremely different tone from their instruments, on occasion inserting staples or other metallic objects into the hammer felts, making more of a harpsichord-type sound, for example. Steinway & Sons usually frowns on this kind of tampering with the hard-won voices of their instruments. Franz Mohr, who started with the firm in 1965 and only recently retired, tells of a set of hammers on a Horowitz piano that he hardened and filed to such a degree that to this day he cannot bear to hear the recording made with the instrument. The sound was too "brilliant," the tone pushed far beyond the limits of that particular instrument, for Mohr's ears. Horowitz, however, was pleased. In my own limited experience, I remember an occasion when Glenn Gould proudly told my father (the two worked together in the 1960s at Columbia Records and became good friends) about some "adjustments" that had been made to one of his pianos, but he forbade him from mentioning it to my mother. She was the Steinway in the family.

No pianist, however, tailored the instrument to his own specifications more than the American iconoclast John Cage. In a series of compositions for the "prepared" piano that he began in the late 1930s, Cage became famous (or infamous, in some circles) for inserting objects in and around the strings to modify the sound of the piano for his unique work. A partial list of the implements that Cage employed reads like a madman's shopping list: screws, nuts, bolts, washers (rubber, metal, and felt), pencil erasers, spoons, plastic cups, paper clips, safety pins, grommets, clothespins, felt and rubber weatherstripping, wire insulation, lamp cord, thumbtacks, aluminum foil, Ping-Pong balls, metal protractors, and "a naked woman" were all specified at one time or another. These compositions are not often attempted by other pianists, much to the happiness of piano technicians the world over, but Cage's own concerts are well documented.

When most piano-savvy people hear the word "voicing," they think of the preparation of the hammers. Indeed, this procedure is crucial, and central to the emergence of a piano's tone. The physical act is really quite simple, requiring only three things: a set of needles, a bottle of "juice" (a mixture of viscous lacquer and lacquer thinner), and the one most difficult to obtain—the expertise of a master tone-regulator.

At the Steinway factory, these artisans are considered the aristocrats of the workforce. Their job is one of the most complex, yet subtlest, in the entire operation. By judicious use of the needles (to break up the fibers, and thereby soften the felt) or application of the juice (to harden it), the tone regulator is the individual who, more than any other,

Voicing tools are simple, but the craftsmanship takes years to acquire.

directly affects the instruments' sound. Not that these masters apply an omniscient standard to the task, or voice an instrument according to their own personal criteria. The tone regulator's task lies somewhere in between: to perceive the potential of each instrument and to secure its full flowering. At the factory the work is done in isolation and at its own pace. A technician such as Mohr, who until 1992 was Steinway & Sons' chief concert technician (in charge of the preparation of all the concert instruments used by the artists who play the Steinway piano exclusively), rapidly becomes the keyboard artist's best friend. Mohr even toured with a few artists to prepare the piano for each concert personally.

This kind of careful attention paid to each piano is one of the hallmarks of the level of craftsmanship at Steinway & Sons, and one of the true sources of the chimerical "Steinway Sound."

The hand-rubbed finish epitomizes

the quality of a Steinway.

FINISHING

PEOPLE WHO DON'T play the piano, or may not even like music, are never-
theless familiar with pianos. Chances are a piano figures somewhere in your childhood
—maybe in your grandmother's parlor, on stage in your school's auditorium, on television or in the movies. The artist at the keyboard of your imagination may range from
Alfred Brendel to Keith Jarrett to Elton John, but the image of the piano is usually consistent. Aside from a Fred Astaire musical or a Las Vegas extravaganza, most people
harbor the same picture of what a piano looks like. They are very large, are usually
shiny black, and take up a great deal of space. If you live with a piano or if you have
ever had the experience of moving one, you may have thought about it as something
other than a musical instrument. This aspect of piano-as-furniture is as necessary to
acknowledge as an 800-pound gorilla would be, if one was in your living room. Since
the late 1800s, when one of the hallmarks of William Steinway's brilliant strategy to
market pianos was to link the instrument with an ideal of civilized living, pianos have
truly become icons in our lives.

The casework, legs, top, and pedal lyre are what we first see when we look at
a piano. They can be considered its clothes, if you will, and are the most furniture-like
elements in a piano's makeup. And as with any piece of fine furniture meant to last
more than one lifetime, great care is taken with the appearance of these parts so as to
enhance the beauty of the object and increase its durability. Whether the finish is the
classic black or a natural grain, the workers at Steinway & Sons begin to prepare these
outer surfaces months before the piano is ready to ship.

Finishing a Steinway, in fact, begins roughly halfway through the process of
making the piano. This is done not only because it's efficient, but also because it allows
the finishing materials to cure more slowly, which results in a better union with the
wood. Finishing wood is an exacting craft that, like so many things about musical

instruments, is more complicated than it may at first appear. Many violin experts say that what really distinguishes the instruments made by Antonio Stradivari from those of his contemporaries is the varnish that he used. While a piano's finish doesn't affect the sound as much as a violin's might, it does affect the statement the owner makes to the world about his or her taste. It can also be an indication of the care the piano maker has shown with the rest of the instrument. Would that the same could always be said for piano owners. Fine violins generally get caressed by soft cloths and laid into plush cases when the music making is done; a piano is lucky if it gets dusted once a month.

Varnish, lacquer, and shellac are the classic transparent wood finishes. These terms are used interchangeably on occasion, which is unfortunate, because each material has a different source, distinct properties, and varying histories. All of them, in one way or another, are found in Steinway pianos. Of the three, lacquer is used in the

Stain brings out the figuring, and helps color-match the wood, on the natural-finish pianos.

greatest quantity—it is the coating on the outside of the case for all the models, black or natural finish. Since before World War I, Steinway & Sons has used different formulations of nitrocellulose lacquer for this purpose. These lacquers, which are basically acid-treated cotton fibers dissolved in volatile solvents, are in a class known as "spirit" finishes. This means that the liquid solvent acts as a dissolving and application medium for the resins (in this case, nitrocellulose), then evaporates completely, leaving a hard film behind. Lacquer has a marvelous history, especially in Asia, where the lacquer tree (*Rhus verniciflua*) grows, the pure sap of which has been used as a finish for fine woodwork, metals, and ceramics for thousands of years. Except for the rare instance, today's lacquer is not derived from this source, but its properties are the same: it is hard, extremely durable, and highly resistant to moisture and temperature variations.

A cascade of mineral oil traps airborne droplets of lacquer in the spraying booth.

Varnish is the broadest classification of these finishes (both lacquer and shellac can be considered varnishes) and is used on the piano's soundboard, where a more flexible finish is desired because the wood vibrates a great deal. There are many different formulations of varnish in the world, but most of them belong in the category of

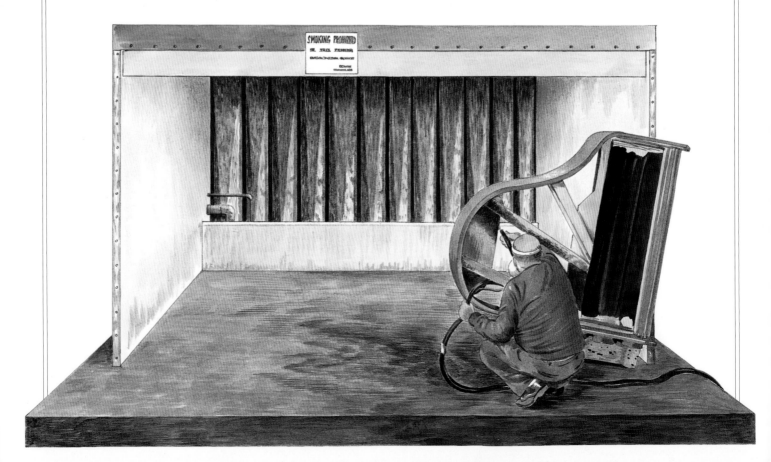

Matching veneers takes time, patience, and know-how.

"oleoresinous" finishes. In these slower-drying coatings, fluid oils and other compounds are mixed with the resins, which chemically react with them as they dry. These types of finishes generally bond more easily to wood, give a more elastic film, and can last a long time with little attention. There is a tremendous variety within the varnishes, with both natural and synthetic ingredients. The formulation that Steinway & Sons uses is proprietary, and an old one. The resins come from fossilized tree sap (amber) that is mined in India.

Of the three, shellac has the most curious origin, is the most old-fashioned, and is the one used least in pianos. It is a spirit finish with alcohol as the solvent, and its resin is a purified form of the natural excretion of a tiny insect, *Laccifer lacca,* that accrues on trees, mostly acacia trees on the Indian subcontinent and in Southeast Asia. The word "lac" derives from both the Farsi and Hindi words meaning "one hundred thousand," which gives you an idea of how many of the little bugs are needed to yield a useful amount of resin. Lac resin was one of the major freight goods in the days of the clipper-ship trade. In addition to wood finishes, it has been used in abrasives, dyes, waxes, hair spray, and cake glaze. Mixed with clay, it was a central component of early recording discs—the brittle 78s, 45s, and even some early long-playing records—as late as the 1950s. At Steinway, shellac, which is known for its sealing properties and dries extremely fast, is used as a foundation coat for some wood types.

All Steinway pianos are available in two different finishes: a "high polish," which has a shiny reflective surface, and a "satin lustre," which is less reflective but more forgiving of fingerprints and smudges. Application of the lacquer is basically the same for the two, with a few variations at the end of the process, depending on which sheen is desired. For the natural-finish pianos, there are also a few extra steps in the bare-wood phase, to ensure that the beauty of the case wood is brought out.

Color matching is also important. There are some parts of the piano, the pedal lyre for example, that do not lend themselves easily to the use of veneer—too many carved or contoured surfaces. In the natural-finish pianos, many of the parts that have to match the veneered surfaces are formed out of solid lumber of the same type, but these pieces of dimension lumber must necessarily come from different trees than the veneer. Sometimes the color will not match exactly, and must be stained.

Stain and fillers are also used to bring out the grain and to prepare the wood for the lacquer. Open-grained woods such as walnut must have their pores sealed before the finish is applied, or it would simply flow beneath the surface instead of building up into the hard coating we expect. These fillers contain minute particles of solids in a watery suspension and are rubbed in by hand, filling the pores of the wood and giving it a light stain at the same time. With many of the exotic woods that Stein-way uses, such as sapele and mahogany, the color of the filler contrasts with the color of the surrounding wood, to heighten the figuring in the grain even more.

A case, however, gets moved around the factory a good deal, and the finishing process dovetails with its manufacture. By the time a case arrives in the belly depart-ment, it has been sanded repeatedly on all surfaces, the wood has been stained and filled, and it has received between four and five applications of sprayed lacquer, with hand sanding in between coats. The black pianos are treated the same as the natural-finish ones from this point—the difference being that a black dye is added to the lacquer. At this stage the finish is tremendously bright, brassy, and usually uneven. Sometimes there are patches of lacquer whose texture resembles the skin of an orange. This is normal. After the piano receives its strings, keyboard, and action, it gets a "rough rub," which knocks down the surface of the lacquer to an even flatness.

After tone regulation and top fitting comes the "final polish," which entails rubbing the surfaces with finer and finer abrasives. Sandpaper and steel wool of higher and higher number (the higher the abrasive number, the finer the grit) are employed by hand, first dry and then lubricated with mineral oil. A series of felt pads are used in conjunction with the oil and a pumice powder to give the ultimate finish. The glossy high polish has a higher degree of reflection, and is given an extra silicone buffing. Strangely, the low-gloss satin finish is more susceptible to scratching—the minute ridges that refract light and give the satin sheen are more easily damaged than the flatter surface of the high-polish finish. The satin finish is considered more desirable for any situation where the piano will be brightly lit, such as a concert hall or television studio. For home use the demand for each finish varies, as fashions in decoration do, but it is possible to have one finish converted to the other.

A few words about caring for the finish on your Steinway. It is not necessary, or recommended, to use wax or any spray-on furniture polish to protect the finish. Lacquer is a tremendously durable substance, and all that is required to preserve the case is a light dusting with a soft, water-dampened cloth. This should be done on a regular basis, and the rubbing motion should always be in the direction of the grain of the wood. It is far more important to keep a piano out of direct sunlight and drafts and as far away from heating and air-conditioning vents as possible. Try to minimize the changes in humidity throughout the year if you can. This way the durable finish of your piano will last as long as it was intended to.

Overleaf: Carnegie Hall, New York City.

ARIA DA CAPO

STEINWAY PIANOS are built to last. This is as true today as it was in the middle of the nineteenth century. The company's reputation rests both on the quality of the instruments they are currently producing and on the durability of the instruments they have made throughout their 140-year history. In light of this fact, some space be should be given to the older ones, because there are a lot of them out there, and any person thinking of acquiring a Steinway will probably consider an antique or previously owned instrument at some point. This is fitting, for many of the basic design elements in the modern piano (such as the scale, the iron frame, and the tubular metallic action frame) have withstood the test of time and can be found in an instrument made in the 1920s as plainly as in one manufactured last week. With a Steinway piano there is also the advantage of knowing that the technology, which was often pioneered by the firm and has since become the industry standard, is combined with strict quality control of materials and workmanship.

However, it is as inevitable with pianos as with people that age will make some mark. For example, the soundboard will lose its crown over time owing to the down-bearing pressure from the strings. This happens in the natural course of events —pianos by both nature and design do not last forever. It is not easy, therefore, to assess the value of a particular piano either as an instrument or as an investment without a certain amount of knowledge. Luckily, that knowledge is available to you either by your own research or through the assistance of a trained professional. If you are interested in an antique or previously owned Steinway piano (indeed, any piano), you can use this book as a starting point, but there are also two avenues open to you: a network of authorized Steinway dealers around the world, and the services of a professional piano technician in your area. The perspective of an independent piano technician (a person who does more to pianos than just tune them) will be of tremendous value in your search, and the assistance of the House of Steinway can give you both peace of mind and an assurance of added value should you choose one of their instruments. If you select an older Steinway that may need repair, you should know that the company does a great deal of restoration work at its New York factory, and they make many of the parts available wherever they are needed.

So how can you tell if the piano you have just seen is worth the price its present owner is asking? That's a simple question that unfortunately does not have a simple answer.

If you are a adept pianist, your own feelings should guide you. If you love a particular piano, that may be all you need to know. That feeling can also guide you in your proper investigation of the instrument's merits. What exactly is it that you love? Does the keyboard have a touch you like? This may indicate that the action is in good shape however much use it has had. Is the case in good condition and does it please you? An important consideration, because you may live with this object for a long time. Is the sound to your liking? This is, perhaps, the crucial question, but any determination of sound quality is an immensely subjective matter. If some things are obviously wrong with this piano, can they be fixed easily?

Even if you don't play the piano, there are a few things you can do to answer these questions. Most important, try to find out the instrument's history—history, that is, in terms of ownership and, more significantly, of maintenance. Ask questions, and examine the instrument. Open the top and take a careful look at the soundboard, strings, and hammer felts. Don't forget to crawl underneath or behind the piano and take a look. Heavy use may be indicated by a number of signs, but it is not necessarily a bad thing. More important is the type of use a piano has had, the maintenance (if any) the piano has received, and the conditions under which the piano has been maintained.

PRACTICE

How you get to Carnegie Hall.

Remember that the primary material of a piano is wood, a substance tremendously responsive to changes in climate but quite durable when kept under the right
conditions. Temperature fluctuation doesn't affect pianos as much as do changes in
humidity, although in many areas of North America, Europe, and Asia these climatic
variations are obviously linked. A seventy-year-old model B that has been lovingly
maintained by someone who plays chamber music on a regular basis may be in better
shape than a twenty-year-old piano that has never been touched and has sat in full
sunlight next to a radiator its whole life.

Of the three avenues readily available to the person who is looking to acquire
a piano (a private sale, a sale from a knowledgeable piano person or qualified dealer, or
a sale from a venue with no specialty in pianos such as an auction), the safest course
may be to stick with a reputable dealer. A Steinway dealer can steer you directly to the
company for parts and restoration work, which is warranteed if performed at the factory. If you are looking at a private sale or an auction, a technician hired for the occasion to accompany you when you inspect the piano could be particularly helpful. In this
instance, too, the firm can assist you. If any repair or restoration work on a piano has
been done at the New York factory anytime in the company's history, they have a
record of it. This is another advantage of dealing with a company with as long a history
and as proud a heritage as Steinway & Sons.

APPENDIX

STEINWAY & SONS currently makes seven models of pianos: five grands and two vertical, or upright, pianos. With the exception of the largest grand piano (the concert grand, model D), they are all available in the classic black ebonized finish, in mahogany, and in walnut. The model D is available in ebonized and walnut only. Additionally, the company's "Crown Jewel Collection" of exotic hardwoods is available for certain models—check with your local Steinway dealer or with Steinway & Sons in New York. All the finishes are available in both high-polish and satin lustre.

For the grand pianos, the model names are as follows (in ascending order of size): S (5′1″, or 155 cm), M (5′7″, or 170 cm), L (5′10½″, or 179 cm), B (6′10½″, or 210 cm), and D (8′11¾″, or 274 cm). A good mnemonic for the model sizes is Small, Medium, Large, Big, and Damn big. The vertical pianos come in two different heights: K (52″, or 132 cm) and 1098 (46½″, or 118 cm).

Recently, the company has been making limited-edition specialty pianos. An "1885" Victorian-style piano, available in models M and B, was released in 1995; and an "Instrument of the Immortals" piano, celebrating the 200th anniversary of the birth of Henry Engelhard Steinway, was made available in 1997.

For prices, financing, and availability, please see your local authorized Steinway & Sons dealer, or you can contact the company directly. In New York City, you can visit the company's showrooms at Steinway Hall, where a complete selection of new and previously owned Steinway pianos awaits your inspection.

For information on factory restoration of older instruments, please contact the company. There is a complete listing of the options available to you if you wish to have your Steinway piano restored, refurbished, or rebuilt with original parts at the Long Island City factory. The addresses are:

Steinway Hall
109 West 57th Street
New York, NY 10019
(212) 246-1100

Steinway & Sons
Steinway Place
Long Island City, NY 11105
(718) 721-2600

GLOSSARY/INDEX

Page numbers are indicated in boldface.

bridge pin A small metal pin embedded in the top of the bridge against which the string presses; there are two for every string in a piano. 51, 109–110

cambium The layer of cells just inside the outer sheath of the stems, trunk, and roots of a tree, which generate both the bark and the useful wood. 37

capo d'astro A metal bar attached to the underside of the iron frame of the piano, used in place of an agraffe in the treble notes to hold the strings in place evenly. 50, 53, 99–100, 106

case The external cabinet parts of a piano. 45, 67, 74–89, 104–109, 117, 128

checks The natural cracks that occur in wood as the material dries, usually found at the ends of logs and boards. 40

cheek warp A term for the distention, over time, of the wooden case of an antique piano constructed without an internal iron frame to withstand the tension of the strings. 92

clavichord An intimate and quiet-sounding stringed keyboard instrument in use from approximately 1500 until the early 1800s, and again in recent years. 13, 14, 15–16

closed-grained The term for lumber with tiny, or nonexistent, pores. Can be finished without the use of pore fillers. 43

color matching The process of staining by which the shade of the wood of the various parts of a natural-finish piano are made to match. 128

compass The range of tones on the keyboard; a modern piano has a compass of seven and one-third octaves, i.e., eighty-eight notes. 64

cope The upper half of the two-part mold used to form a piano's iron frame. 96, 97, 98–99

crown A slight dome given to the soundboard in order to withstand the down-bearing pressure of the strings and maintain its proper shape. 61, 132

damper A felt-covered wooden action part that lifts off the strings when the key is pressed and falls back when it is released, thereby deadening the sound. 53, 57

Diaphragmatic (soundboard) A thinning of the edges of the soundboard so as to increase the potential for vibration where it attaches to the case. 61

double repeating (action) A mechanism that allows a note to be struck a second time before the key is released to its full upright position. 66

drag The lower half of the two-part mold used to form a piano's iron frame. 96, 98-99

duplex scale A design scheme where the ends of the piano's strings are sized so as to vibrate in sympathy with the main portion, resulting in a fuller sound. 51, 53

English action Since the mid-1800s, the dominant grand piano action design scheme wherein the hammers are oriented so that their heads are located on the far side of the pivot point. 19, 64-65

flask In casting a piano's iron frame, the metal framework that is placed over the master form and filled with compacted sand to create the mold into which molten metal is poured. 96

flitch A complete section of tree trunk that has been sawed into thin pieces of veneer and is shipped as one unit. 48

fraizing The process of trimming the dimensions of a grand piano rim to the proper size. 84, 108

fundamental vibration The basic pitch to which a note is tuned, such as F-flat, F-sharp, etc. 50-51, 57

gray iron The mixture of iron ore and composite materials that is melted together and poured into a mold to create a piano's metal frame; also known as cast iron. 93, 96, 97, 99

hammer The felt-covered wooden mallet that strikes the strings, thereby creating sound. 50, 52, 53, 57, 66, 69-70, 117, 119-120, 133

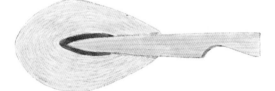

hammer dulcimer A multistringed instrument with a characteristic ringing sound, played with hand-held beaters that strike downward upon the strings. 12, 13-15, 65

hammer head The felt-covered wooden action part that hits the strings. 50, 64, 66, 69, 133

hardwood The type of lumber that comes from a broadleaf, flowering tree. 38-40, 42, 44-45, 48

harp An alternate name for the iron frame fastened to the piano's inner rim to which the strings are attached; it enables the strings to be held under tremendous tension. 21, 51, 91-100, 102, 104-112

harpsichord A stringed keyboard instrument, forerunner of the piano, first described in 1397 and still in use. 12, 14, 16, 119

heartwood The physiologically inactive portion of a tree's trunk or limb. Located near the center of the tree and useful for lumber. 37-38

high polish The name for the most reflective, glossy finish available on Steinway pianos. 128-129

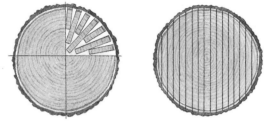

hitch pin The metal pin at the terminal end of the piano string that holds the string in place. 51, 53, 56, 93, 97, 99, 100, 106, 109, 113

inner rim The wooden structural part of a grand piano rim to which the soundboard and iron frame are attached. 76-85, 106-108

Ivorene The plastic compound that replaced ivory and ebony on the keys in the modern piano. 72

keybed A wooden panel to which the keyboard and action are attached; it slides in and out of the piano for easy access. 60, 66-67

keylid The curved, hinged wooden cover that

pivots down to protect the keyboard when a piano is not in use. 46, 85

lacquer A varnish used to coat a wooden surface for an especially hard, glossy, durable finish. 100, 125-126, 128-129

lamination (laminate) The process of bonding multiple layers of thin strips of wood (laminates) into one integral piece. Also applicable to the use of veneer. 61, 77-79, 81-84

listing A piece of cloth such as felt, woven through the strings at the far end of a keyboard instrument to dampen the vibration of that portion. 16

music desk The wooden, hinged support in front of the keyboard that holds the player's music. 46, 85, 87

node The exact point between vibrations of partial segments of a string, occurring at measurable intervals along a string's length. 57

oleoresinous finishes Varnishes made of resins mixed with chemical compounds and fluid oils. 127

one-piece overstrung iron frame Since the 1850s, the dominant design scheme of a

grand piano's internal iron frame. 23–25, 53, 92–93

open-grained The term for lumber with large, absorbent pores. Must be treated with pore fillers before application of wood finish. 43, 128

outer rim The external portion of a grand piano's wooden rim. 23, 76–85

overstringing A design scheme where the bass and treble strings cross over each other, adding length and creating a larger sound. 23, 25, 53, 92–93, 113

overtone A higher tone faintly heard above the fundamental pitch of a note, resulting from the vibration of a partial segment of the string. 56–57

partial segments In a piano string, the portions whose vibrations give rise to higher, fainter tones than the notes' fundamental pitch. 50–51, 56, 57

pedal lyre The wooden part that descends from a grand piano case and holds the pedals in place. 44, 60, 107, 128

pianoforte The original name for an early version of the piano, in use from approximately 1700 to 1850. 8, 12, 16–20, 22, 116

pin block The laminated wooden plank at the keyboard end of the piano in which the tuning pegs are embedded; also known as the wrestplank. 84

pitch The particular, relative position of a tone in a musical scale as determined by its frequency of vibration, such as C-flat, C, C-sharp, etc. 16, 56–57

pith The very center of a tree's limb, trunk, or root. 37

plain-sawn Refers to lumber milled along the grain; produces boards of varying, but decorative, quality. 39, 41, 48, 77

prepared piano A piano that has been tampered with to affect its sound, by inserting objects in and around the strings. 120

quartersawn Refers to lumber milled axially against the grain; produces the most durable, strongest boards. 39, 41–42, 59

rim The curved, laminated wooden structural framework that supports the soundboard, iron frame, and keybed, etc., in a grand piano. 45, 61, 74–89, 93, 104–108

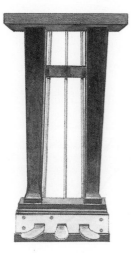

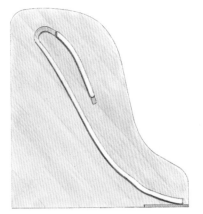

sapwood The physiologically active portion of a tree's trunk or limb. Located just beneath the bark, but not extending to the tree's center, and generally useful for lumber. 37, 38

satin lustre The name for the least reflective, buff finish available on Steinway pianos. 128–129

scale In a piano, the basic layout of the strings, bridge, and hammers relative to one another and to the overall size of the instrument. 52–56

seasoning The natural drying process by which moisture in wood is reduced. 40

shellac A varnish used to penetrate and seal some varieties of wood. 126–128

softwood Name for type of lumber that comes from an evergreen, coniferous tree. 38–40, 45–46

soundboard A large, domed, spruce panel that amplifies the vibration of the strings and gives the piano its volume. 43, 46–49,

50–61, 93, 102, 104–109, 117, 126, 132–133

speaking length The principal segment of a piano's string, whose vibration gives the instrument the greater part of its sound. 15–16, 53, 56–57

spirit finish Varnishes whose resins are suspended in a volatile fluid that evaporates after application. 126

sympathy (sympathetic vibration) A natural phenomenon where a string will vibrate when a nearby string is excited, even though it has not been struck itself. 57

taking the bearing The process of lowering the top surface of the wooden bridge so that the angle of the strings brings the proper downward pressure onto the soundboard. 106–110

tangent One of a series of upright blades, usually made of brass, which are fixed to the end of a clavichord's key and pivot upward to strike the string when the key is depressed. 15, 16

top The hinged wooden panel that covers the strings of a grand piano; can be partly opened to expose the strings for projection of sound, or removed altogether. 46, 48, 60, 85

tubular metallic action frame A metal armature to which the individual action mechanisms that transmit the pressure on the keys to the strings are fastened. 66–68

varnish A broad term for a number of different kinds of smooth coatings applied to a wooden surface, which can be built up into an attractive, durable, protective film. **43, 112, 126–127**

Viennese action An early design scheme for a grand piano's action mechanism wherein the hammer head is located on the keyboard side of its pivot point. **19, 64–65**

voicing The adjustment of the action pieces and the hardness of the hammer heads to achieve the best, most even sound from the piano; also known as tone regulation. **116–121**

whippen The central action part that allows the hammer to fall from the strings after striking them. **66–67, 68, 70**

wrestplank The laminated wooden plank that sits at the keyboard end of the piano in which the tuning pegs are embedded; also known as the pin block. **44–45, 50, 84, 100, 108**

Name	Address / Notes	Month
Howard	St. Paul Minn. for M. Ives	Nov
R. Bass	Colorado Springs Col. Ctr Gerrit Smith	July
McCormick	Port Jervis N.Y. ph. to P.E. Farnum Port Jervis N.Y.	Feb
Schenck	Proprietor of Westminster Hotel	Feb
Raynor	15 West 36 Str	Apr
from Hamburg to Steinway & Sons London		July
Steinway	C/o Joh. Schroeder Hamburg	Sept
T.A. Kenefick	78 East 54 St Joseph O. Fisher	Oct
Steinert	New Haven Conn. 5.16 - 5 av Dec 15/71	Sept
Rinecke	47 East 78 Str	Sept
206 W 29 St ph. to Mrs. A.B. Jennings Short Hills (this side Summit N.J.) Brooklyn		June
& Son Providence R.I. del. to J.H. Richardson		Apr
from Hamburg to C. Hartwig Hamburg		
Steinway	C/o Joh. Schroeder Hamburg	Aug
Steinert	New Haven Conn.	Oct
Cottier	Buffalo N.Y.	Jan
Miles	9 East 66 Str.	Mch
Guy	San Francisco Cal.	Nov
52 Lodge Pt. ph. to W.P. Brownsville by New Orleans Str. "Lone Star"		Jan
Backus (of San Francisco Minstrels) 246 West 44 St. Sept. 28. 1882.		
Sacca N.Y. first ph. to Glen Cove L.I.		June
Baldwin	426 Bloomfield Str. Hoboken N.J.	Jan
Upton Hamburg to St Johns London exchanged June 14/81		May
Steinway C/o Joh. Schroeder Hamburg		Nov
Hilliard Herbert Barlow E 13th St Oct 10/41		
A. McIntosh 110 Lefferts Place Brooklyn		Nov

147

Number	Oct	Style	Sye	Wood	from	Factory	
43510	7/3	G	4'8"	Eby	Nov 24/80	w.p. hammers.	
43511	7/3	G	4'8"				
43512	7/3	G	4'8"				
43513	7/3	G	4'8"				
43514	7/3	G	4'8"				
43515	7	B	6'8"			not fin. Not Var.	
43516.	7	A	6'				
43517	7	A	6'			es during fire Mar.	
43518	7	A	6'				
43519	7	A	6'.			board plates, key block screws,	
43520	7	A	6'			le case with bottom work. strung	
43521	7	F	5'4½"				
43522	7	F	5'4½"				
43523	7	F	5'4½"	Rosd Jan 5/81		w.p. hammers	
43524	7	F	5'4½"	Rosd Dec 29/80		w.p. hammers.	
43525	7	F	5'4½"	Rosd May 3/81		for.	
43526	7	F	5'4½"	Rosd Jan 8/81		w.p. hammers.	
43527	7	A	6'	Rosd Nov 1/80		2 pedale unfnd	